Virginians at Home

Williamsburg in America Series

II

The second in a series of popular histories
focusing on the roles of Williamsburg and Virginia
in the eighteenth century

Virginians at Home

FAMILY LIFE IN THE EIGHTEENTH CENTURY

By Edmund S. Morgan

THE COLONIAL WILLIAMSBURG FOUNDATION
Williamsburg, Virginia

Morgan, Edmund Sears.
Virginians at home; family life in the eighteenth century.
Williamsburg, Va., Colonial Williamsburg [1952]
99 p. illus. 21 cm. (Williamsburg in America series, 2)
1. Virginia—Soc. life & cust.—Colonial period.   1. Title.
P234.W7W7   vol. 2   917.55   52–14250 ‡
ISBN 0–910412–52–9

Fifth printing, 1977

PRINTED IN THE UNITED STATES OF AMERICA

CONTENTS

v

ILLUSTRATIONS

Virginians at Home

INTRODUCTION

Virginia in 1776 had grown and changed in many ways since her founding in 1607. She was no longer a small settlement huddled around a swampy little town; rich plantations lined the banks of her rivers for a hundred miles into the interior, until the first waterfalls interrupted navigation. The planters maintained their own wharves, and ocean-going ships moved up and down the rivers collecting tobacco for English and European smokers and bringing back in return the English manufactures which helped to make life in the Virginia Tidewater a provincial counterpart of life in England.

Beyond the Tidewater rose the Virginia Piedmont, gentle, rolling slopes which were already covered with farms and plantations. Here there were no convenient waterways to connect the settlers directly with England. The tobacco and wheat grown in the Piedmont had to be carted laboriously over rough roads to reach the ships which would carry them to market. Life was not as easy as in the Tidewater. Settlers were more isolated from each other, and had to rely more on themselves than the planters who could step aboard a ship and travel from their own doorsteps to any place in the world.

Even more isolated was the Shenandoah Valley, which lay beyond the Great Blue Ridge. The Valley had been

settled for the most part, not by the Englishmen who occupied the Tidewater and Piedmont, but by German and
Scotch-Irish farmers who had moved down from Pennsylvania and who still sent their products back to Philadelphia and Baltimore to market. They did not build
great plantations, but then not all Virginians in the Tidewater and Piedmont were great planters either. For every
planter with his gang of slave laborers there were many
small farmers. They were Virginians too; so were the
slaves who worked on the plantations, and the servants
who were earning their freedom, and the merchants and
artisans of Fredericksburg and Norfolk. Even the shiftless "lubbers" along the Carolina border were Virginians,
although fastidious gentlemen like William Byrd of Westover did not like to recognize them as such.

In other words Virginia was not only a vast territory,
but a place where, in the course of a history almost as
long as that of independent America today, a complex
society had already developed. Some Virginians were so
poor that they did not even have a roof to cover them.
Others were surrounded by servants and slaves who provided them with every luxury. At the top of the social
scale stood the great planter, owner of a mansion on one
of Virginia's noble rivers, where he lived with his family
and his entourage of servants; owner also of other plantations which he entrusted to the direction of overseers;
member of the House of Burgesses, or perhaps of the
Governor's Council; owner of a house in Williamsburg,
where he and his family lived during fashionable "Publick Times" when the legislature was in session. Between
this man and the farmer in the Valley there was a wide
gulf in wealth, in education, and in occupation, but they

were both a part of the same society, and both joined in fighting a war for their independence.

When that war was over, Virginia had changed. She was still able to provide great statesmen for the new nation, but at home her prosperity was gone, and although she eventually recovered it in part, she never again presented the unique pattern of colonial times. The following pages are an attempt to reconstruct some of that pattern, to show what life was like in the homes of eighteenth-century Virginia.

The woodcuts reproduced throughout this book and on the dust jacket are from *A Little Pretty Pocket-Book*, published by Isaiah Thomas at Worcester, Massachusetts, in 1787, and are used through the courtesy of the Reserve Division of the New York Public Library.

His parents loved him as much as any modern parents could.
Members of the Page family of Rosewell, painted by an
unknown artist, possibly Gustavus or John Hesselius.

I

GROWING UP

An infant coming into the world in Virginia during the eighteenth century had a good deal more reason to cry about it than one who arrives in any part of the United States today. Not that he found himself among unfriendly or indifferent people. His parents would love him as much as any modern parents could, but since they knew nothing of modern medicine and sanitation, they were by our standards woefully unprepared to care for him. They knew nothing about germs and viruses or how to fight them. Their baby would have to take his chances against diphtheria, diarrhea, and a host of other terrors, and his chances were not very good. The parents would often be more of a hindrance than a help. They might very well aggravate an illness by administering some potion which today nobody in his right mind would think of drinking himself, let alone giving to a sick child. Infancy, in fact, was so dangerous a condition in the eighteenth century that relatively few children survived. It was common for a father and mother to see most of their children die before they were able to walk or talk.

If, however, a child lived through the first few years, he could look out on a world which had its faults but which might well afford him a long and happy life. Much would depend, of course, on how he had chosen his parents. If he was so unfortunate as to have a mother with a black skin, life had little in store for him: he would probably have to spend it working for somebody else. He might be taught to expect nothing more, but he would always have beside him the example of other children with a happier fate who automatically received everything that he had lost before he was born. If, on the other hand, he had free parents who lived in a cabin on the frontier, he would grow up to the tune of hard work, but he would see his work bring rewards, and he would enjoy the kind of childhood which with all its dangers and excitements has become the envy of modern boys and girls to whom it is denied. If, finally, he had the good luck to have parents who owned a great plantation or a good house in Williamsburg, he might look forward to everything that the world could offer: a life of security and comfort with entertaining and sophisticated companions.

Leaving for a moment the children who were born into slavery, we may get a glimpse into the lives of the other children of eighteenth-century Virginia from the letters, diaries, and newspapers which have been preserved in libraries, in historical societies, and in the attics of houses where those children grew up. From these records we may reconstruct a picture of childhood in Virginia as it was two hundred years ago.

A modern parent thrust back into colonial Virginia would find that bringing up children presented the same problems to parents—and to children—as it does today. "Spare the rod and spoil the child" is an adage which we are apt to associate with all ages prior to our own; we assume that modern psychology and "progressive" education have challenged that notion for the first time. It is exception of the grammar school at the College of William and Mary, there were no schools supported by public funds. Most Virginians, therefore, who wished to give their children a school education, had to send them to private schools either in the colonies or in England. In the early years of the colony, those who could afford it usually sent their children to England, placing them under the care of a friend or business acquaintance there. William Fitzhugh in 1698 sent his eleven-year-old son to George Mason in Bristol, with a letter saying, "Sir, by this comes a large and dear consignment from me, the consignment of a son to your Care and Conduct." Fitzhugh suggested that the boy be placed at a school he had heard of, three or four miles outside Bristol, but concluded, "Now Sir I have told you my mind and how I would have him managed If I could, I must at last say in generall terms, that I refer the whole to your discreet and prudent manage, assuring myself that if you are pleased to undertake the trouble, you will do by him as if he were a child or relation of your own, and shall without more saying refer him wholly to your Conduct, and hope within a week after his arrival you will contrive him to his business, whats necessary for him, either for books, cloathes or now and then a little money to buy apples, plums &c., is left solely to yourself and all charges shall be punctually answer'd you and thankfully acknowledged."

Children were sometimes sent to school in England at a very early age. Ursula Byrd was shipped off in 1685 at the age of four, under the care of a ship's captain, and seventy-five years later three more Byrd children were at school in England. The eldest described himself in a letter to his grandmother as being four feet, four inches tall, his brother Jack, eleven, as "half a head shorter than me, and Tom is half a head shorter than him."

Throughout the eighteenth century, though less often in the latter half, Virginia boys and girls of wealthy families continued to cross the ocean for an English education. English schools even advertised in the Virginia newspapers. In 1766 the Reverend B. Booth advertised his academy at *"the seat of the late Lady Mollineux's at Woolton, five miles from Liverpool,"* where he boarded young gentlemen and taught them English, Latin, Greek, writing, arithmetic, merchants' accounting, geography, navigation, astronomy, surveying, mathematics, and drawing—all for twenty-one pounds a year. Entrance fees, laundry, music, dancing, and fencing were extra. In 1769 Aaron Grimshaw advertised an academy at Leeds, where young gentlemen were "genteely boarded, and diligently instructed in English, the classics, modern languages, penmanship, arithmetic, merchants accounts, mathematics, modern geography, experimental philosophy, and astronomy, for Twenty Guineas *per annum*, if under twelve years of age." A postscript to the advertisement added: "Drawing, music, and dancing are extra charges. Due regard is paid to the young Gentlemens health, morals, and behaviour."

The postscript was probably dictated by the recognition of a growing reluctance on the part of Virginians to send their children to England. Though there were obvious advantages to an English education, there were also increasingly obvious disadvantages. The eighteenth century was an era of great licentiousness and corruption in England, and the boys and girls who were educated there frequently returned with dissipated health, corrupt morals, and bad manners. Moreover the expenses involved always amounted to more than a parent could anticipate; the children learned extravagant tastes from their companions and spent money at a rate beyond that which they could afford. Consequently, however fashionable and however broadening it might be, an English education came to be looked upon less and less favorably in Virginia. Landon Carter in 1770 observed, "I believe everybody begins to laugh at English education; the general importers of it nowadays bring back only a stiff priggishness with as a little good manners as possible." Richard Henry Lee in 1785 declared that he never knew an instance of a "Young Lady Educated in England" who could live happily in Virginia, and William Nelson turned down the offer of his London correspondent, John Norton, to look after the education of Nelson's son. "I am extreamly obliged," he wrote to Norton, "by your kind offers of Civility and Friendship, if I should send my Son Hugh to England: and the more so as I can reply upon the Sincerity of these Professions; but I have no Thoughts at present of sending him, and he no great Inclination to such a Voyage indeed the Temptations to Expence and Dissipation of Money and Time are too great for our Estates here; Especially as the Improvements of our youth are Seldom answerable to Such great Expences as they often incurr."

Many wealthy Virginians, who could have afforded to send their children to England, agreed with Nelson that an English education was not worth the price, that in fact it was of doubtful value at all. For parents who felt this way a possible alternative was to send their children to one of the boarding schools which had been established in Virginia and Maryland. There was for example the grammar school attached to the College of William and Mary in Williamsburg. Or if one wished to escape the temptations offered in even that small metropolis, there were other schools such as Somerset Academy on the Eastern Shore, described in the *Virginia Gazette* on February 23, 1769. Here the total cost annually amounted to only seventeen pounds per student. The whole academy was housed in a building 62 by 20 feet where forty scholars and two masters lived together. According to the account in the *Gazette*, "the scholars are taught the rudiments of English grammar, orthography, or the art of spelling, and some portion of time is spent every week to perfect them in writing. They are instructed in the *Latin and Greek languages*, and may be taught the various branches of the *arts and sciences*, such as geography, logick, navigation, surveying &c." The academy was "remote from any neighboring town, which might interrupt it by diversions, or infect it with vicious examples; and yet not so solitary, but what it enjoys a variety of good company." Here the youth of Virginia might acquire a good education "without spending their fortunes, or distressing their parents."

Even so well recommended a school as this had its disadvantages, as all boarding schools do. Children who were separated from their parents and subjected to the company only of schoolmasters and of other children like themselves missed the beneficial influences of home life. To overcome these drawbacks and at the same time to give their children adequate schooling, many wealthy Virginians resorted to a method of education which became customary on the larger plantations of the region: the maintenance in the family of a private tutor. For those who could afford it, this was by far the most desirable solution to the educational problem. Yet it was not always easy in Virginia to find the right kind of man to fill the position of tutor. He should be a gentleman, for he would take dinner with the family and participate in family activities almost as a social equal. He should have a good education, preferably a college education, for he must be able to give instruction in Latin, the language of scholars and a necessary accomplishment for any gentleman who pretended to culture. A man with these qualifications was difficult to find, for a Virginian who could afford such a preparation did not need to earn his living by teaching other men's children. Sometimes planters in search of tutors advertised in the newspapers, as Landon Carter did in 1772, offering fifty pounds a year to any gentleman who would teach six of his grandsons grammar, writing, and arithmetic, "besides boarding as a companion at all leisure hours, provided he can conform to the rules of a private family nothing averse to an easy freedom, not carried into any excess." Carter was unable to get the kind of man he wanted but finally hired the son of a local parson with the understanding that he should have a salary of only thirty pounds a year "until he convinced me he was a proper person for such a concern." Landon Carter's nephew, Robert Carter of Nomini Hall, got his tutors through President Witherspoon of Princeton. Other planters sought assistance from friends in England. Richard Corbin wrote in 1766 to a London correspondent: "I am greatly in want of a tutor to my children, it gives me pain to see them misspending the precious moments of their youth. I must earnestly intreat you therefore to procure me an honest man well skilled in the languages, that writes a good hand, and is

throughly acquainted with arithmetick & accounts. This
is so interesting to me that I flatter myself you will exert
your endeavors to engage a gentleman qualified in all
respects for this business and send him over by the first
ship."

It was necessary to exercise the greatest care in the
selection of a tutor, because the children of the family
would spend most of their waking hours under his
supervision. The school day was a long one. At Belvedere
the children were at their studies from six in the morning
to noon, with an hour out for breakfast, and from three
to six in the afternoon. At other plantations the schedule
was about the same. The children went off to school
as soon as they were dressed and were not finally dismissed until evening. Maria Carter at Sabine Hall wrote
a description of her day in a letter to her cousin at
Cleve in 1756: "Well then first begin, I am awakened
out of a sound Sleep with some croaking voice either
Patty's, Milly's, or some other of our Domestics with
Miss Polly Miss Polly get up, tis time to rise, Mr. Price is
down Stairs, and tho' I hear them I lie quite snugg till my
Grandmama uses her Voice, then up I get, huddle on my
cloaths & down to Book, then to Breakfast, then to
School again, & may be I have an Hour to my self before
Dinner, then the Same Story over again till twi-light, &
then a small portion of time before I go to rest."

When the children of any plantation had been roused
out of bed in the morning, whether by servants, grand-
parents, or parents, they usually trooped off to a school
building in much the same way that children do today,
for most planters who employed a tutor set aside a
separate building for him to keep school in. At Belvedere
it was a "neate litle House 20 foot long and 12 foot

wide" which stood by itself at the end of a row of planting. At Nomini Hall the school occupied one room of a building in which the tutor and the boys of the family slept. The boys tumbled out of bed when the tutor did and as soon as they were dressed went downstairs to the schoolroom. The girls slept with their mother and father in the mansion house, which was located about a hundred yards distant, and had to walk over to the schoolhouse. Sometimes they arrived before the tutor was ready to begin school and the children had a brief time to chat and play together as they do in the schoolyard today before the bell rings.

A plantation school in session must have looked very much like the one-room country school of our own day, for the children all attended at the same time. Young men preparing for college would be studying Latin and Greek in the same room where their younger brothers and sisters were learning the alphabet. At Nomini Hall, when Fithian arrived in the autumn of 1773, he found eight pupils. Ben, seventeen years old, was reading Sallust and studying Latin and Greek grammar; Bob and Harry, the latter a nephew of Mr. Carter, were fourteen and studied English and arithmetic; Priscilla, thirteen, was reading the *Spectator* and beginning arithmetic; Nancy, eleven, was reading out of the spelling book and beginning to write; Fanny, nine, was simply reading in the spelling book; and Harriot, five, was just beginning the alphabet. John Harrower at Belvedere had three children in his charge, apart from those sent by neighboring planters: Edwin, ten, was just beginning two-syllabled words in the spelling book; Bathurst, six, was still on the alphabet (but three years later he had completed a reading of both the Old and New Testaments of the Bible), and William, only four, was just beginning. There was also a daughter, Hannah Bassett, but Harrower did not mention how old she was or whether she was studying with him.

To teach each child separately while maintaining schoolroom discipline must have required ingenuity and adaptability on the part of the tutor, but the individual attention which each child received was a compensation for whatever defects the system might have. Each child could be guided according to his temperament and capacities in the directions which would be most fruitful for him. This may sound like an idealization of an archaic system of instruction, for probably most teachers, then as now, lacked either time or ability to understand the individual personalities of their students. Yet Philip Fithian showed a sympathetic interest in all the children under his charge. Moreover this interest was exactly what the accepted educational precepts of the time demanded. The idea that each student should be considered as a separate educational problem is no invention of twentieth-century progressive education. It was a commonplace in the eighteenth century that what was then called the "genius" of every child should be considered in planning his program of study. The American colonists were fully aware of "the Absurdity of setting every Boy to write Verses, and pursuing the same Tract, whatever be the Inclination, Capacity, Fortune, or intended Profession of the Scholar." Although this absurdity was doubtless practiced then as much as it is now, there is no reason to suppose that the tutors on Virginia plantations were any worse than other teachers, and with only a small number of pupils under their care they were certainly in a position to give attention to every student's inclination and ability. A good example of such individual attention was John Harrower's success with the deaf-and-dumb son of a neighboring planter, who attended school at Belvedere along with the other children. In five months' time Harrower brought the boy to the point where "he can write mostly for anything he wants and understands the value of every figure and can work single addition a little."

Although it was recognized that each child had a different personality, it was a generally accepted belief that the capacities of a girl could never equal those of her brothers. A girl was not expected to go beyond the study of reading, writing, and arithmetic. There was no sense in bothering her head with Greek and Latin, for she would never be able to undertake the advanced liberal education for which these were the foundation. The idea of admitting a woman to a university would have been ridiculed in the eighteenth century, just as Eliza Custis, Martha Washington's granddaughter, was laughed at by her stepfather when she observed that she "thought it hard they would not teach me Greek and Latin because I was a girl—they laughed and said women ought not to know those things, and mending, writing, Arithmetic, and Music was all I could be permitted to acquire."

While the boys of a family were busy with Latin and Greek, or perhaps with the mysteries of accounting or law, the girls had to study the social graces and domestic skills of a housewife. Girls probably did not attend school with the tutor for as many years as boys, for they had much to learn that a tutor could never teach them. They must know how to manage a household the way their mother did, and they must learn polite accomplishments such as fancy needlework and playing a musical instrument. Sometimes a governess was called in to instruct them in these mysteries and in the fine points of social behavior. Sometimes they spent a year or two at a girls' boarding school; and sometimes their mothers taught them. There were, besides, itinerant instructors who traveled from plantation to plantation giving music lessons. Music was considered a highly appropriate accomplishment for a well-bred young lady, and even for a well-bred young man. But more important than music, for boys and girls alike, was dancing.

Dancing was taught in the same way as music, by itinerant masters. When the dancing master arrived, both boys and girls were freed from the schoolroom and assembled for the day in the ballroom. This was doubtless a welcome relief from the routine of reading, writing, and arithmetic, but it was no mere frolic. The children had to go through their paces with precision and grace, for the dancing master demanded as strict a discipline on the dance floor as the tutor did in the schoolroom. Fithian described a session of the dancing school at Nomini Hall:

After Breakfast, we all retired into the Dancing-Room, & after the Scholars had their Lesson singly round Mr Christian, very politely, requested me to step a *Minuet;* I excused myself however, but signified my peculiar pleasure in the Accuracy of their performance—There were several Minuets danced with great ease and propriety; after which the whole company Joined in country-dances, and it was indeed beautiful to admiration, to see such a number of young persons, set off by dress to the best Advantage, moving easily, to the sound of well performed Music, and with perfect regularity, tho' apparently in the utmost Disorder—The Dance continued til two, we dined at half after three—soon after Dinner we repaired to the Dancing-Room again; I observe in the course of the lessons, that Mr Christian is punctual, and rigid in his discipline, so strict indeed that he struck two of

the young Misses for a fault in the course of their performance, even in the presence of the Mother of one of them!
And he rebuked one of the young Fellows so highly as to
tell him he must alter his manner, which he had observed
through the Course of the Dance, to be insolent, and wanton,
or absent himself from the School—I thought this a sharp
reproof, to a young Gentleman of seventeen, before a large
number of Ladies!

Though the regular school day on the plantation was
a long one, it was considerably broken by a three- or
four-hour recess in the middle of the day, when the
boys and girls could escape to more important things
than school. Fithian observed that each of his pupils had
his own special diversions; "Bob, every day at twelve
o-Clock, is down by the River Side with his Gun after
Ducks, Gulls &c.—Ben is on his Horse a Riding, Harry,
is either in the Kitchen, or at the Blacksmiths, or Carpenters Shop. They all find places of Rendesvous so
soon as the Beell rings, and all seem to choose different
Sports!"

The girls had their pastimes too, and rushed off when
the bell rang to help the cook bake a pie, or to dress
their dolls, or to look after their pets. A plantation was
a great place for pets. Many planters kept herds of tame
deer in a stockade and sometimes the children made pets
of the fawns. Some girls kept squirrels in cages, and of
course there were countless cats and dogs. Little Sally
Fairfax recorded with indignation the death of a cat
which had become too familiar with one of her father's
slaves. "That vile man Adam," she wrote, "at night killed
a poor cat of rage, because she eat a bit of meat out of
his hand & scratched it. A vile wretch of new negrows,
if he was mine I would cut him to pieces, a son of a gun,
a nice negrow, he should be killed himself by rites." The

girls at Nomini Hall were fond of playing house. Fithian used to watch them, "sometimes tying a String to a Chair & then run buzzing back to imitate the Girls spinning; then getting Rags & washing them without water—Very often they are knitting with Straws, small round stocking, Garters &c—Sometimes they get sticks & splinter one end of them f[o]r *Brushes*, or as they call them here *Clamps*, & spitting on part of the floor, they scrubb away with great vigor—& often at a small game with Peach-stones which they call *checks*." One day Fanny, aged ten, and Harriot, aged six, "by stuffing rags & other Lumber under their Gowns just below their Apron-Strings, were prodigiously charmed at their re-semblance to Pregnant Women!"

During these free hours and in the evening after five o'clock the children also saw something of their parents. Sometimes a father would go hunting or fishing with his son, or a girl might help her mother arrange the table, or the whole family might enjoy a barbecue or fish fry by the river. The relationship between parents and children at these times must have been a pleasant one, for the parents had usually turned the whole respon-sibility for discipline over to the tutor. It was the tutor who decided whether a boy should be permitted to visit a friend or go to a horse race. It was the tutor who concerned himself with all the squabbles and all the pranks of children with which modern parents normally must deal. Fithian's journal indicates that children's capacities for getting into trouble were much the same in the eighteenth century as now. One day it would be a catch-as-catch-can fight, as on February 8, 1774, when Fithian wrote, "Before Breakfast *Nancy* & *Fanny* had a Fight about a Shoe Brush which they both wanted—

Throughout the eighteenth century, though less often in the latter half, Virginia boys and girls of wealthy families continued to cross the ocean for an English education.

This eighteenth-century engraving shows an English school-master reprimanding one of his scholars.

*"After Breakfast, we all retired into
the Dancing-Room."*

A family group painted by Charles Philips (1708-1747), now
hanging in the Governor's Palace, Williamsburg.

Fanny pull'd off her Shoe & threw at Nancy, which missed her and broke a pane of glass of our School Room. they then enter'd upon close scratching &c. which methods seem instinctive in Women." Another time it was Bob's staying out all night or Nancy's clipping off her eyebrows and then maintaining that somebody else had done it while she was asleep. The tutor had to deal as best he could with these and the thousand other inescapable vexations of childhood that frequently cause friction between parents and children. Sometimes his responsibility was divided with a governess, who took charge of the girls, but in any case the parents were relieved of the unpleasant task of punishing their children or of denying them things they wanted but could not be permitted to have. Sometimes the parents could even intercede for the children, as when Mrs. Daingerfield rescued her son from a spanking by Harrower. Though the father later upheld the tutor's authority, the mother doubtless appeared a heroine in the eyes of the child.

Thus the tutorial system had a double advantage: it kept the children at home, away from the corrupt influence of the outside world, and at the same time it freed the parents from the most irksome responsibilities of parenthood. No wonder tutors were in demand. Yet the number of families who could afford such a luxury was inevitably small. The majority of Virginians were not plantation owners but small farmers. Probably less than half of Virginia's families in the eighteenth century owned slaves at all, and those who held a sufficient number to render them affluent were a small minority even of the slaveowners. It was only this small minority who could afford either to hire tutors or send their children to boarding school.

It was out of the question for most families to send their children to school at all unless they happened to live in the neighborhood of one of the handful of free schools. Sometimes a group of farmers or small planters would get together and set up a school at some point convenient for all. They might hire a schoolmaster, or perhaps one of their number would purchase an indentured servant who had the proper qualifications and rent his services to the rest of the group, each member paying his share. Schools of this kind were usually established in old tobacco fields which had lost their fertility and been abandoned. Although a good many children were educated in these "old-field schools," the number of Virginia children who ever saw the inside of a schoolhouse must have been a relatively small proportion of the population. Even in New England, where free schools were established by law, it is doubtful that a majority of children attended them, and in Virginia, where the schools were much scarcer, the proportion was undoubtedly smaller.

The education of most boys and girls was limited to training in the skills by which they would make their livings; those who, in addition, learned their letters and figures, must have done it either in their own homes or in someone else's home.

One may ask why any child would have been likely to learn such things in another person's home. This question would not have occurred so readily to anyone living in colonial days. It had been a common custom in England, at the time when the first colonists left, for parents to turn over the upbringing of their children to some other family. The origins of this custom are not entirely clear, for it was practiced by families who could not have done it for any conceivable financial reason. Children of gentlemen were frequently placed as servants in the families of other gentlemen. One of the reasons seems to have been that parents were afraid of spoiling their own children; they did not trust themselves with the knotty problems of discipline although they had no hesitation in assuming responsibility for the children of others. Whatever the reason for it, this custom was continued by the colonists, particularly by the northern colonists, but to some extent by the southerners too. Although the practice seems to have been dying out in the eighteenth century, at least as far as the upper classes were concerned, we have seen that some wealthy Virginians entrusted the education of their children to friends in England. There is also an amusing instance, recorded by William Byrd, of an English girl whom he found serving a friend of his in Virginia. This girl, according to Byrd, was a baronet's daughter, "but her Complexion, being red hair'd, inclin'd her so much to Lewdness, that her Father sent her, under the care of the virtuous Mr. Cheep, to seek her fortune on this Side the Globe."

It was among the lower classes, however, that the practice of "putting out" children in other families was most common, and here the motives for it are clear. Sometimes the family was too poor to support all its children, in which case both boys and girls might be bound out as apprentices in other families. More often the motive was not directly economic—not, that is, to relieve the family of the burden of feeding and clothing the child—but educational. Children were placed in other families as apprentices, in order to learn a trade. A man with a large family of sons and daughters could not expect to set each of them up in the world with a business or a farm. To be sure, land was cheap, and probably most boys learned to follow the plough on their father's farms and then moved to land of their own when they grew up. But many parents thought it desirable for their sons who would one day be supporting families of their own, to learn a trade, and the way to learn a trade was by becoming apprentice to a man who practiced it. Apprenticeship had been for centuries the only method of acquiring industrial skills and it remained the only method until the advent of the technical high school and institute of technology of our own day.

To become an apprentice was to assume for a number of years the position of a servant in another family. The master of the family could command the apprentice to any task and could punish him if he disobeyed. The master was, in fact, as responsible for his apprentices as he was for his own children. He must feed, clothe, and house them and see that they behaved. Children might be bound out as apprentices at almost any age, but the normal age for a boy was fourteen, in order that, after serving a term of seven years, he might become free when he reached the age of twenty-one. If he were apprenticed before or after the age of fourteen his term usually ran until he was twenty-one anyhow. It is not easy at this distance to discover much about the life of an apprentice in eighteenth-century Virginia, though we may safely make a few conjectures. There was probably no social stigma attached to the position, for in spite of the fact that the apprentice had to accept the status of a servant, apprenticeship was a normal method of education and had always been so regarded. How hard the apprentice had to work depended much upon the family in which he was placed. If his master were relatively affluent he might have an easier life than he would in a household where the members of the family were obliged to work long, hard hours for themselves. Though apprentices sometimes complained to the courts that they were overworked, the judges were usually unsympathetic. The only complaints to which they would give attention were those to the effect that the master failed to give instruction in the trade that the apprentice was supposed to be learning, or that the master failed to give instruction in reading or writing.

In the seventeenth century reading and writing were not a compulsory part of an apprentice's training, but they became so in the eighteenth century. This does not mean that an apprentice devoted much time to book learning. Probably most of his instruction in letters was rather haphazard. A tutor from a near-by plantation might come at odd hours and give a few lessons, or the apprentice might be sent for a term to an old-field school, but more often the master himself must have undertaken the job in his spare time. For the most part the apprentice was kept busy at the tasks assigned him, becoming familiar as he worked with every phase of the master's craft. By the time his term was up he would be ready to hang out his own shingle as a cooper or carpenter or blacksmith or to work for wages as a skilled artisan, either for a great planter or for another master of his craft in one of the towns. By this time also, he was ready to think about getting married.

The boy who had grown up on his father's farm would probably have reached this step earlier. A farm boy is usually ready to start life for himself before he reaches the age of twenty-one, and with a plentiful supply of land in the back country it was easy enough for a young man to move out and establish his own household. The son of a planter, on the other hand, was usually kept in leading strings for a longer time. A boy could not marry without his father's consent until he reached the age of twenty-one, and most parents who could afford it preferred to continue their sons' education until they reached that age. The general scarcity of adequate instruction was even more acute at this higher educational level. A tutor could prepare a pupil for college, but there was no substitute for college itself, and here again Virginia offered a limited choice. The College of William and Mary had been opened as early as 1698, and every year many Virginia boys of the best families matriculated there, but during the last decades of the colonial period the college was in bad condition. Robert Carter told Fithian that he had "known the Professors to play all Night at Cards in publick Houses in the City, and . . . often seen them drunken in the Street!" William Randolph went so far as to provide in his will that his son should not be sent there on any account whatever. Other parents sent their children to Edinburgh, Oxford, or Cambridge or to the northern universities. Princeton, founded in 1746, was particularly popular with the Virginians, in spite of its Presbyterian bias, and so was the college at Philadelphia (later to become the University of Pennsylvania). One Virginian even contemplated moving to Philadelphia because the college there was so superior to that in Williamsburg. William Reynolds, a Virginian visiting Philadelphia in 1772, wrote to John Norton, "Mr. Savage seems determined upon moving to this place about Spring twelve Month, the prevailing Motive wth him I believe

is the Education of his Children the Colledge here being
under exceeding good Regulation, & that in our Colony
quite the reverse, to the Shame of the Virginians be it
spoken."

The deficiencies of William and Mary and the distance
of other universities probably prevented many Virginians from attending college who would otherwise
have done so. Sometimes as an alternative to a university
education, and sometimes in addition to it, an able young
man would seek training in the law. This was considered
a highly suitable accomplishment for a gentleman, especially in a colony like Virginia where gentlemen were
in full control of the local government, and where every
gentleman was expected to take an active part in politics,
whether in the Governor's Council, the House of Burgesses, or the county courts and parish vestries. The best
possible legal training was to be had at the Inns of Court
in London, but a satisfactory alternative was to serve an
apprenticeship with a leading attorney in the colony or
to read at leisure the great English jurists. After 1779
it was possible to attend lectures in law at William and
Mary, where George Wythe had become the first
professor of law in an American college, but even
before that time Virginia gentlemen were remarkably
well read in the law, a fact which may help to account
for their extraordinary contributions to the political
and constitutional development of the United States.

Another alternative to a university education, for
those whose parents stood a little lower in the social
scale, was to serve an apprenticeship to a planter, with
a view to becoming an overseer. Landon Carter used
to instruct young men in this profession and even pay
them something as wages in the last years of their ap-

prenticeship. Mr. Christian, the dancing master who visited Nomini Hall when Fithian was there, bound his son to Landon Carter, as the latter recorded in his diary, October 3, 1772: "Mr. Christian came here last night and brought his son Raleigh to be bound to me. He is 15 years old, and but small. I got him indented till he is 20, which will be the 7 of Sept. 5 years hence. I am to make him a capable steward over Gentleman's estate if I can, and am to give him £10 a year the two last years of his time." Thus apprenticeship might provide vocational training even in the upper ranks of society.

When a parent had taken care of his children's education, whether by private tutors, by schools and universities, or by apprenticeship, he had discharged most of the obligations of a parent. One thing remained. No good parent could rest easy until he had seen his children through the most important single step in their careers, marriage.

2

GETTING MARRIED

For most young people getting married was simple enough. The couple discovered one another in the usual ways, obtained the consent of their parents, had the banns published in the parish church, and were married by the local minister. They could forget their parents' consent—as far as the law was concerned—if the girl was over sixteen and the boy was twenty-one, but of course it was not good taste for children to proceed in these matters without their parents' advice. Custom in Virginia demanded what in some of the northern colonies the law required, that a man get the consent of a girl's parents before he presumed to propose marriage. Marriage was not entirely a private affair: it was family business, and the other members of a family had a right to say something about who should be admitted to their circle. However, the small farmers and artisans who made up the great majority of the population of Virginia gave their children a broad freedom in these matters. A poor man with a large family could not expect to leave much to his children when he died, nor could he afford to provide his daughter with a dowry or his son with a marriage portion. His children would have to make their way in the marriage mart as best they could; if they fell in love with other boys and girls who owned as little property as themselves, no one would be a loser by the match. It was a matter of courtesy and decency for them to consult their parents, but where no great fortunes were at stake on either side there was little reason for parents to stand in the way of their children's wishes.

For the children of wealthier families, in Virginia as in every other part of the world, marriage was less simple. Boys and girls who could expect to come into an inheritance were not allowed to share their fortune with anyone who happened to please their fancy. They must take care to maintain and increase the portion allotted them. An eighteenth-century New Englander put the central problem of marriage eloquently if bluntly when he wrote that there was little to be said about marriage except this, that "if a man should be [so] unhapy [as] to dote upon a poore wench (tho' otherwise well enough) that would reduce him to necessity and visibly ruine his common comforts and reputation, and at the same time there should be recommended to him a goodly lass with aboundation of mony which would carry all before it, give him comfort, and inlarge his reputation and intrest, I would certainly, out of my sense of such advantage to my friend, advise him to leave the maid with a short hempen shirt, and take hold of that made of good bag holland."

If it be supposed that such crude sentiments were peculiar to New England, one may recall the case of Captain John Posey, a neighbor of George Washington, who once wrote to Washington that he was contemplating paying his debts by marrying an "old widow woman." The only drawback to this match was that the widow was "as thick as she is high" and addicted to regular spells of drunkenness, during which she was said to be of a "viliant Sperrit." Although the Captain finally went to debtors' prison rather than face the valiant spirit of such a wife, there is no reason to suppose that his neighbors would have considered the match dishonorable. Money was so proper a consideration in the choice of a mate that the newspapers, in announcing weddings, sometimes stated the sums of money involved. For example, there was no need for the gossips in Williamsburg to wonder how much of a dowry Betty Lightfoot brought Beverley Randolph in 1737, because the *Virginia Gazette* stated plainly that she was "an agreeable young Lady, with a Fortune of upwards of 5000 £." Who would not be agreeable with a fortune of five thousand pounds?

Though marriage was supposed to be connected somehow with love, it was also an investment, and anyone who entered upon it with a good share of capital was expected to take care that his partner should also contribute a proper share. A man who owned nothing but the shirt on his back might match where he chose, with nothing to lose, but anyone who had property must invest it wisely if he wished to keep it.

Since wisdom has never been the distinguishing mark of youth, the parents of families in the higher ranks of society frequently took an active part in planning their children's marriages. A man who had spent a lifetime in accumulating a fortune did not wish to see his son squander it on a maid with a short, hempen shirt, nor did he wish to see his daughter hand it over to a man who could not otherwise support her in a manner befitting her birth. Moreover parents who had a position of dignity to maintain did not wish to be disgraced by connections with persons of ill fortune or ill repute. Sometimes parents arranged the whole business, with the children playing a comparatively passive role. More often, probably, a boy informed his father that some young lady had caught his fancy, whereupon the father, if he approved, would negotiate with the girl's parents. Thus Thomas Walker wrote to Colonel Bernard Moore:

May 27th, 1764

Dear Sir:

My son, Mr. John Walker, having informed me of his intention to pay his addresses to your daughter, Elizabeth, if he should be agreeable to yourself, lady and daughter, it may not be amiss to inform you what I feel myself able to afford for their support, in case of an union. My affairs are in an uncertain state, but I will promise one thousand pounds, to be paid in 1766, and the further sum of two thousand pounds I promise to give him; but the uncertainty of my present affairs prevents my fixing on a time of payment. The above sums are all to be in money or lands and other effects, at the option of my son, John Walker.

I am Sir, your humble servant,

THOMAS WALKER

Colonel Moore replied the next day:

May 28, 1764

Dear Sir:

Your son, Mr. John Walker, applied to me for leave to make his addresses to my daughter, Elizabeth. I gave him leave, and told him at the same time that my affairs were in such a state that it was not in my power to pay him all the money this year that I intended to to give my daughter, provided he succeeded; but would give him five hundred pounds more as soon after as I could raise or get the money, which sums you may depend I will most punctually pay to him.

I am, sir, your obedient servant,
BERNARD MOORE

Probably not all negotiations were as smooth as these. Evidence from other colonies suggests that parents frequently bargained over the amounts to be given their children with all the enthusiasm they might have devoted to a horse trade. Samuel Sewall of Boston recorded in his laconic style an account of how he arranged his daughter's marriage with Joseph Gerrish: "Dine with Mr. Gerrish, son Gerrish, Mrs. Anne. Discourse with the Father about my Daughter Mary's Portion. I stood for making £550.doe: because now twas in six parts, the Land was not worth so much. He urg'd for £600. at last would split the £50. Finally Febr. 20. I agreed to charge the House-Rent, and Difference of Money, and make it up £600."

In Virginia as in New England there seems to have been a rule of thumb by which such bargaining was regulated: the girl's parents were expected to contribute about half of what the boy's parents did. Thus in 1705 Daniel Parke, a Virginian residing in London, wrote back to John Custis, whose son was courting Parke's daughter in Virginia:

Sir: I received yours relating to your son's desire of marrying my daughter, and your consent if I thought well of it. You may easily inform yourself that my daughter Frances will be heiress of all the land my father left which is not a little nor the worst. My personal estate is not very small in that country, and I have but two daughters, and there is no likelihood of my having any more, as matters are, I being obliged to be on one side of the ocean and my wife on the other. I do not know your young gentleman, nor have you or he thought fit to send an account of his real and personal effects; however, if my daughter likes him, I will give her upon her marriage with him, half as much as he can make it appear he is worth.

Evidently the children, even of wealthy parents, might take the initiative in arranging their own marriages, leaving the financial details to their parents. Such an arrangement presumed that a boy or girl would have sense enough to choose a partner of proper social standing. Occasionally, then as now, children thwarted the prudence and snobbishness of their parents by marrying for love with persons of low degree. William Byrd of Westover related the "tragical story" of a girl who married her uncle's Irish overseer. "Besides the meanness of this mortal's Aspect," Byrd wrote, "the Man has not one visible Qualification, except Impudence, to recommend him to a Female's Inclinations. But there is sometimes such a Charm in that Hibernian Endowment, that frail Woman cant withstand it, tho' it stand alone without any other Recommendation. Had she run away with a Gentleman or a pretty Fellow, there might have been some Excuse for her, tho' he were of inferior Fortune: but to stoop to a dirty Plebian, without any kind of merit, is the lowest Prostitution. I found the Family justly enraged at it; and tho' I had more good Nature than to join in her Condemnation, yet I cou'd devise no Excuse for so senceless a Prank as this young Gentlewoman had play'd."

When a girl or boy was of age, there was little that a parent could do to prevent matches of this kind, beyond disinheriting the unruly child. Sometimes even this was impossible. If the estate were entailed to the eldest son, the father could not prevent him from inheriting it in any case. Sometimes the father could not even disinherit his daughters. John Paradise, when he married Lucy Ludwell, gained control of a large estate, but he found that his interest in the property was only for his own lifetime and that he could not control its inheritance by their children after his death. As a result he was unable to prevent his daughter's marriage to an impecunious Italian nobleman whose charms had won both the girl's affections and her mother's good will. If a boy or girl were under age, it was possible to prevent a marriage, but even then a couple might elope and persuade some gullible minister that they were of age. Occasionally the patrons of the *Virginia Gazette* read advertisements like the one inserted by Benjamin Bowles on August 27, 1756:

> Whereas *Sarah Holman*, a Niece of mine, under Age, and to whom I am Guardian, hath lately made an Elopement from me, and, as I believe, with an Intent to marry one *Snead* (alias *Crutchfield*) and as I think it will be greatly to her Disadvantage, this is to give Notice to all County-Court Clerks not to grant them Marriage License, and to all Ministers not to marry them by Publication of Banns. I not knowing what Part of the Colony they may resort to, to accomplish their Design, am obliged to make Use of this Method to prevent them.

Doubtless most boys and girls who had been brought up in the elegant manner were content to abide by the rules of the game and seek their mates among those who were as genteel—and as wealthy—as themselves. There were plenty of opportunities for the children of the first families to meet each other at the balls and entertainments which formed part of the high life of colonial Virginia. Probably many a match began in the formal banter which passed between couples engaged in the steps of a minuet or a country dance. The gentleman would pour out a string of extravagant compliments while the lady blushed and protested. Soon perhaps the gentleman would come visiting the lady at her father's plantation, and if his character and financial qualifications were in order, might eventually ask for her hand. At this point both he and the lady were obliged to follow a ritual which required considerable dramatic skill. Though everyone agreed that marriage must be a union of properly proportioned worldly fortunes, nevertheless convention demanded that the actual proposal take place in an atmosphere of almost religious formality. The lady must be approached with fear and trembling as a kind of saint, the lover prostrating himself either literally or figuratively before her, while she betrayed great surprise and distress at the whole idea of marriage and agreed to consider the proposition only after much protestation. Sometimes a lover could not bring himself to undertake so excruciating a performance in person and would commit his proposal to writing, but even then the lady must go through the form of protest before agreeing. A charming letter, from Anne Blair of Williamsburg to her sister Mrs. George Braxton, describes a young Virginia belle's reaction to a letter of proposal:

She was in a little Pett, but it was a very becoming one, let me tell you. A glowing blush suffused o'er her face attended with a trembling, insomuch that in extending her arm to reach me *the creature's insolence* I thought the Paper would have fallen from her Hand. The emotions I saw her in did

*The lady must be approached with fear and
trembling as a kind of saint.*

This illustration is from a little book entitled *Various Kinds
of Floor Decorations* (London, 1739). It is displayed here
not as an example of the proper kind of floor covering but of
the proper approach to a lady.

*If she lived in the Valley, she would probably see
the land prosper.*
A view in the Shenandoah Valley at harvest time.

not fail of exciting the curiosity in me natural to all our Sex, so that a dog would not have caught more eagerly at a bone he was likely to lose than I did at the fulsome stuff (as she call'd it) tho' must own on perusal was charmed with the elegance of his stile: and I dare say he might with truth declare his love for her to equal that of Mark Anthony's for Cleopatra. She thought proper to turn his letter back again with just a line or two signifying the disagreeableness &c. &c. of the subject . . . . There are several others Dancing and coopeeing about her, may they scrape all the skin off their shins stepping over the benches at Church in endeavoring who sho'd be first to hand her in the Chariot.

One need not suppose that every girl could play her part as well as this, but she was expected to make the attempt. Between themselves, of course, girls did not have to maintain the pretense and doubtless discussed their feelings and prospects as frankly as they do today. Anne Blair in another letter describes what one must assume to be a mock duel fought by two local belles over one of the officers of a British man-of-war stationed at Hampton Roads in 1768:

"How stand your hearts Girls," I hear you ask? Why, I will tell you, mine seems to be roving amidst dear variety; and notwithstanding there is such Variety do you think Betsy Blair and Sally Sweeny does not contend for *one?* Betsy gave her Toast at Supper Mr. Sharp (a Lieutenant on Board the Rippon) Miss Sally for awhile disputed with her, at length it was agreed to decide it with pistols when they should go to bed. No sooner had they got upstairs than they advanced up close to each other, then turning short round, Back to Back, marched three steps forward and fired; so great was the explosion and so suffocating the smell of Powder, that I quitted the Room, till by Betsy's repeated shouts I soon learned she had got the better of her antagonist. Both survive.

The ladies occasionally objected to the conventions which demanded that they act without regard to their inner feelings. The *Virginia Gazette* on October 22, 1736, carried a set of verses entitled "The Lady's Complaint," in which the author deplored the greater freedom which custom gave to men.

> They plainly can their Thoughts disclose,
>   Whilst ours must burn within:
> We have got Tongues, and Eyes, in Vain,
>   And Truth from us is Sin.
>
> * * * *
>
> Then Equal Laws let Custom find,
>   And neither Sex oppress;
> More Freedom give to Womankind,
>   Or give to Mankind less.

Perhaps it was the author of these verses who a week later inserted this advertisement in the paper:

WHEREAS *a* Gentleman, *who, towards the latter End of the Summer, usually wore a Blue Camlet Coat lin'd with Red, and trim'd with Silver, a Silver-lac'd Hat, and a Tupee Wig, has been often observ'd by* Miss Amoret, *to look very languishingly at her the said* Amoret, *and particularly one Night during the last Session of Assembly, at the Theatre, the said* Gentleman *ogled her in such a Manner, as shew'd him to be very far gone; the said* Miss Amoret *desires the* Gentleman *to take the first handsome Opportunity that offers, to explain himself on that Subject.*
        N.B. She believes he has very pretty Teeth.

Such boldness was certainly bad taste, unless, as is quite likely, the advertisement was merely a printer's prank. In any case the ladies' complaints brought no change in custom. It was never leap year in colonial Virginia, and a self-respecting young woman of quality had to play out the role of aloof and unwilling goddess before she could gracefully take the part of a bride.

The wedding itself, when it finally occurred, was performed by the local minister according to the form prescribed in the Book of Common Prayer. It commonly took place at the home of the bride, usually in the afternoon. The friends of the bride prepared a handsome feast to follow the ceremony. There might also be a ball, and since balls frequently lasted for more than a single evening, the couple might have to put up with the wedding guests for several days.

The humbler people of Virginia, who had no time for the elaborate ritual of a genteel courtship, made as much of the wedding celebration as their wealthier neighbors did. In the frontier region known as the Valley, the German farmers who had come down from Pennsylvania used a wedding as the occasion for a frolic in which most of the community took part. In fact if neighbors or relations were not invited, they might take revenge by cropping the manes and tails of the horses of the wedding company while the festivities were in progress. Here, as in the Tidewater region, the wedding took place at the home of the bride. On the morning of the appointed day the friends of the groom, both male and female, assembled at the home of his father, in time to reach the home of the bride by noon. The whole party rode together with great hilarity until within a mile of their destination. Then at a given signal they raced to the bride's home at full gallop, the first to arrive winning "black Betty," a bottle of liquor.

The ceremonies took place at noon and were followed by a feast, during which the guests attempted to steal the bride's shoe. Four of the prettiest girls and four of the handsomest young men were appointed to defend her, each of them being presented with a beautifully embroidered white apron as a badge of office. Since these "waiters" had not only to defend the bride but also to serve the dinner, it was not impossible for a dexterous guest to succeed in stealing the shoe. If this happened the bride had to pay a forfeit of a bottle of wine and could not dance until she had done so.

The dancing, which began as soon as the dinner was over, lasted until morning. About nine or ten o'clock in the evening, when the music and dancing were in full swing, a party of young ladies quietly took the bride up a ladder to the loft and put her to bed. A delegation of young men then took the groom up. There followed a ceremony called throwing the stocking, in which the bridesmaids stood in turn at the foot of the bed, their backs toward it, and threw a rolled stocking over their shoulders at the bride. The groom's attendants did the same, aiming at the groom. The first to succeed in hitting the mark was supposed to be the next one married. Toward morning refreshments, including "black Betty," were sent up the ladder to the bridal pair. The festivities did not end with the morning but continued until the company were so exhausted that they needed as many days to recuperate as they had spent in reveling.

When the last of the guests had departed and the bride accompanied her husband to the home he had prepared for her, she had to face the hard work which marriage entailed. If her husband was a simple farmer, living remote from shops and stores and seeing very little money in the course of a year anyhow, her hands would have to make many of the things that another woman could purchase, and do the things another woman could have done for her. She would have to spin cotton, flax, and wool, weave and knit them, sew, look after the hogs and poultry, milk the cows, make butter and cheese, bake bread, clean the house, and get the meals, besides bearing and rearing children. Sometimes she had to do part of her husband's work as well as her own. At hay and harvest time she would swing a scythe and help to gather in the grain; in the spring she might stand behind a plow, and in summer she would help to trim the weeds with a hoe. She and her family would have plenty to eat, but except for a wedding celebration or a house-raising or a harvesting bee, there would be little time for anything but work.

If she lived in the Valley, the wife of a hard-working German farmer, she would probably live to see the land prosper and in later life, after the Revolutionary troubles had passed, might at least enjoy security. If she lived on the southern frontier of Virginia, the region adjoining North Carolina, we may judge that her life was much harder. According to William Byrd, the women of this region got little help from their husbands in keeping the family alive. Byrd described the men as lazy and shiftless: "They make their Wives rise out of their Beds early in the Morning, at the same time that they lye and Snore, till the Sun has run one third of his course, and disperst all the unwholesome Damps. Then, after Stretching and Yawning for half an Hour, they light their Pipes, and, under the Protection of a cloud of Smoak, venture out into the open Air; tho' if it happens to be never so little cold, they quickly return Shivering into the Chimney corner. When the weather is mild, they stand leaning with both their arms upon the corn-field fence, and gravely consider whether they had

best go and take a Small Heat at the Hough [Hoe]:
but generally find reasons to put it off till another time.
Thus they loiter away their Lives, like Solomon's Slug-
gard, with their Arms across, and at the winding up of
the Year Scarcely have Bread to Eat." Byrd came across
one family without even a roof on their house, so that
whenever it rained, they had to take refuge in a hay-
stack.

Life on a great plantation was never like this, but
not even the greatest of Virginia matrons could boast the
leisure of a woman comparably situated today. Though
she might have all the servants she could ask for, most of
them would be unwilling workers, indentured servants
who looked forward only to the day when they would
be free, or slaves who had nothing to gain by their service.
To manage a large mansion with such a crew was no
small task in itself. It meant constant attention to see
that the jobs assigned to every servant were completed.
Getting a meal on the table was a major operation, for
the housewife never knew how many mouths she must
feed. Hospitality demanded that anyone who passed
the plantation, whether friend or stranger, be invited
to dine, and guests might stay for several days or even
weeks. The Carter family at Nomini Hall consumed in
one year 27,000 pounds of pork, 20 beeves, 550 bushels
of wheat (to say nothing of corn, which was eaten
exclusively by servants and slaves), 4 hogsheads of rum,
and 150 gallons of brandy.

On special occasions, when the family gave a ball or
entertainment for the neighboring planters, the prepa-
rations were on a grand scale, and the lady herself might
work in the kitchen along with her helpers. Little Sally
Fairfax recorded in her diary on December 26, 1771,

that "mama made 6 mince pies, and 7 custards, 12 tarts, 1 chicking pye, and 4 pudings for the ball." There were doubtless many times when the mistress of a plantation felt that it was easier to do a job herself than entrust it to an irresponsible servant. Fithian noted one evening after a visit to a neighboring plantation, that "When we returned about Candlelight, we found Mrs Carter in the yard seeing to the Roosting of her Poultry." Mrs. Carter also managed the gardens which supplied her kitchen, and though there is no record in her particular case, it is known that on most plantations the lady of the house also took care of the sick, both white and colored.

Although her household duties required active hard work, the mistress of a plantation was obliged to maintain all the appearance of leisure. Fithian was much impressed with Mrs. Carter's grand manner. She was entirely accustomed, he said, to "the formality and Ceremony which we find commonly in high Life." Not only did she preside graciously over the dinner table, but she dressed with precise elegance. Fithian was perceptibly shocked one day, after he had been with the family for several months, by what he described as "a Phenomenon, Mrs Carter without Stays!" Fashion demanded that ladies of Mrs. Carter's position be constantly enclosed in stays; not only that, but they must wear clothes which were clearly designed to hamper any sort of useful activity. This was the era of hoop petticoats, which made so simple a task as walking from one room to another a problem in navigation. At the time of Fithian's employment by the Carters, a memorable achievement of the clothes' designers was exhibited by an English governess who had just arrived on a neighboring plantation: Fithian describes with dismay the extent to which the latest fashion would cut the ladies off from the outside world: "Her *Stays* are suited to come up to the upper part of her shoulders, almost to her chin; and are swaithed round her as low as they can possibly be, allowing Her the liberty to walk at all: To be sure this is a vastly modest Dress!"

There were evidently compensations to being a farmer's wife. While Mrs. Carter sweltered in her stays in the Virginia summer, Molly, who worked beside her husband with a hoe, had at least the advantage of wearing only a linen shift and petticoat, with feet, hands, and arms bare.

The lady who graced the table of a Tidewater mansion and the housewife who cooked by the fire in a one-room cabin were equally subject to their husbands' authority. A single woman might own property, contract debts, sue and be sued in court, and run her own business, but a married woman, so far as the law was concerned, existed only in her husband. If he died before she did, she was entitled to a life interest in a third of his property, but during his lifetime he had the use of all her real property and absolute possession of all her personal property. He even owned the clothes on her back and might bequeath them in his will. Though he was not given power of life and death over her, he was entitled to beat her for any faults she exhibited. He had the right to order the lives of her children, even to the point of giving directions in his will for their management after his death. Her duty was submission to whatever he commanded. When William Byrd III, absent in the armed service, directed his wife to send her ailing baby to her mother-in-law at Westover, she replied

Although her houshold duties required active hard work, the mistress of a plantation was obliged to maintain all the appearance of leisure.

The lady dressing fish in this English engraving is not the mistress of a plantation but she is certainly making every effort to maintain the appearance of gentility.

The ladies were laced within an inch of their lives.

"Tight Lacing, or Fashion before Ease," an engraving, from
a picture by John Collet, published in London about 1777.

submissively, "I am very sorry you have limited Poor, sweet Otway, so that he has but a short time to stay with me. . . . But Sir, your Orders must be obeyed whatever reluctance I find thereby." The force of convention was strong upon this point, so strong that it could even overcome religious prejudice. In 1708 Ann Walker, an Anglican married to a Quaker, objected in court to having her children educated as Quakers, but the Court, while acknowledging her own freedom to worship as she chose, instructed her not to interfere in any way with the instruction of her children, even forbidding her to expound any part of the scriptures to the children without her husband's consent. Such complete support for the husband's authority is all the more remarkable in view of the fact that the Anglican Church was the established church of Virginia, to which all the members of the court doubtless belonged.

In the face of all this testimony, it may be rash to suggest that eighteenth-century Virginia had as great a share of hen-pecked husbands as any other society. Yet one may venture a guess that women found ways to assert their power in spite of all the laws and conventions with which the men sought to protect themselves. One gets an inkling of this from the account by William Byrd II of a visit to one of his overseers on a remote plantation. Byrd found many things out of order and reprimanded the man for his neglect. "I also let him know," says Byrd, "that he was not only to Correct his own Errors, but likewise those of his Wife, since the power certainly belong'd to him, in Vertue of his Conjugal Authority. He Scratcht his head at this last Admonition, from whence I inferred that the Gray Mare was the better Horse."

It is hard to know in how many families the gray mare was the better horse. In Byrd's own family it was often touch and go as to who should have the upper hand. On May 23, 1710 he wrote in his diary "I had a great quarrel with my wife, in which she was to blame altogether; however I made the first step to a reconciliation, to [which] she with much difficulty consented." Six weeks later he wrote, "In the afternoon my wife and I had a terrible quarrel about the things she had come in [that is, things she had had imported from London] but at length she submitted because she was in the wrong," and he added with insufferable smugness, "For my part I kept my temper very well." He did not say, however, whether Mrs. Byrd's purchases were sent back to England. On October 12, the same year, he noted that "After we were in bed my wife and I had a terrible quarrel about nothing, so that we both got out of bed and were above an hour before we could persuade one another to go to bed again." The next year on February 5, when the family was preparing to go to Williamsburg, there was another quarrel because Mrs. Byrd wished to pluck her eyebrows. "She threatened she would not go to Williamsburg if she might not pull them; I refused, however, and got the better of her, and maintained my authority." Byrd evidently regarded this as something of a triumph. In spite of all the restrictions which bound a woman to the will of her husband it seems not unlikely that the colonial dame wielded as great a control over her husband as any modern wife does over hers.

There was, as a matter of fact, a good reason why women should have had something of an advantage over men in colonial Virginia: women were a scarce commodity. The first settlers of Virginia had been men, adventurers out to better their fortunes in the New World. Once the settlement was established women were sent over by the shipload in order to make wives for the colonists, and later immigrants included women as well as men. But in any colonization men are apt to predominate; they go first to prepare the way. By the eighteenth century most of the inhabitants of Virginia were of native birth, but there was always a stream of immigrants pouring into the land, and among these always a preponderance of men, so that throughout the colonial period there were never enough women to go around. Those men who had been left out in the marital game of musical chairs were constantly on the lookout for wives. A girl seldom had the opportunity to get beyond her teens before she married. William Byrd wrote to a friend in England that his daughter Evelyn, aged twenty, was "one of the most antick [antique] Virgins" he knew of. And a widow, it would appear, scarcely had time to attend her husband's funeral before another suitor would be after her.

In view of this scarcity of women it would not be surprising if the Virginia wife managed to exert more authority in the household than custom and law allowed her. There are many examples in the records of wives who displayed an independence altogether out of keeping with what the etiquette books demanded. There was Sarah Harrison, who married Dr. James Blair, the founder of the College of William and Mary. At her wedding when the minister reached the part of the ceremony where she was supposed to promise obedience to her husband, she said "No obey," upon which, according to the only account of the wedding that has been pre-

served, the minister, a Mr. Smith, "refused to proceed
and the second time she said No obey and then he refused again to proceed. The third time she said No
Obey; yet the said Mr. Smith went on with the rest of
the ceremony."

Another hot-tempered wife who refused to bow
before her husband's superiority was Mrs. John Custis.
She and her husband lived a hectic life at Arlington on
the Eastern Shore, where they sometimes went for weeks
without speaking to one another. On one occasion when
they were out driving the husband proceeded to drive
the carriage into Chesapeake Bay. When his wife asked
him where he was going, he answered "To Hell,
Madam." "Drive on," answered Mrs. Custis, "any place
is better than Arlington." When he had carried his
whim so far that the horses began to lose their footing,
Mr. Custis turned toward shore again, saying to his wife,
"I believe you would as lief meet the Devil himself, if
I should drive to hell." "Quite true, Sir," she replied, "I
know you so well I would not be afraid to go anywhere
you would go." John Custis managed to have the last
word, for when he died, long after his wife, he left in-
structions to inscribe on his tomb:

> Beneath this Marble Tomb lies the Body
> of the *Hon. John Custis, Esq.*
>
> * * *
>
> Aged 71 Years, and yet lived but seven years,
> which was the space of time he kept
> a bachelor's home at Arlington
> on the Eastern Shore of Virginia.

A wife who found her husband unbearable could not
hope to escape from him by a divorce, for there was no

court in Virginia with authority to grant one. The courts did occasionally arrange legal separations, in which the husband was required to provide the wife with an independent maintenance, but the common remedy for an unbearable husband was to run away, either to another man or back to mother. The *Virginia Gazette* often carried advertisements inserted by irate husbands warning all merchants to grant no further credit to their eloped wives. Most of these advertisements give no clues as to why the wife had eloped, but occasionally a wife answered the advertisement with another which indicated that the fault was none of hers. When Filmer Moore announced the elopement of his wife, she countered with a notice which read:

As my Husband *Filmer Moore* has publickly said his Mother would sooner live in a hollow Tree than with me, and has removed me to my Father's House, with Promise to come and live with me until I could be better provided for (which I can prove by divers Witnesses) but since has falsified his Word, and has perfidiously absented, and kept himself from me these six Months, without any Provocation from me (*so that he has eloped from me, and not I from him*) I do here declare that I intend to remain in the Situation he has placed me until he does come and account for the undeserved scandalous Treatment which I have received at his Hands. And as he has forbid all Persons from crediting or entertaining me, I can prove this to be only Spite and ill Will; for I have not run him in Debt one Farthing, nor removed from my Station wherein I was placed by him.

ELIZABETH MOORE

In spite of such episodes there is no reason to suppose that colonial Virginia had more than its share of unhappy marriages, and it certainly had its share of happy ones. Among the letters from the eighteenth century which have been preserved are many which passed between husband and wife and which reveal as much warmth and tenderness as anyone could ask. Theodorick Bland, absent with the American armies in New Jersey in the winter of 1777, wrote back to his wife: "For God's sake, my dear, when you are writing, write of nothing but yourself, or at least exhaust that dear, ever dear subject, before you make a transition to another; tell me of your going to bed, of your rising, of the hour you breakfast, dine, sup, visit, tell me of anything, but leave me not in doubt about your health. . . . Fear not, my Patsy—yes, 'you will again feel your husband's lips flowing with love and affectionate warmth.' Heaven never means to separate two who love so well, so soon; & if it does, with what transport shall we meet in heaven?"

3

SERVANTS AND SLAVES

Our daily lives are enough like those of our forebears to enable us to visualize sympathetically the vicissitudes of a colonial wife or the perplexities of colonial parents. It is when we consider the problems which the men and women of colonial Virginia faced in dealing with those who worked for them that we realize what a tremendous gap of custom separates us from those days.

For us the word "servant" has the limited connotation of someone who helps to do the housework. Two hundred years ago servants did perform all domestic tasks but also a much wider range of activities. Their work not only increased the comfort and convenience of the family but provided it with income as well. Servants helped the master of the family in his home workshop, where they produced by hand many of the goods which today are turned out by machines in factories. They were not outsiders but an essential part of the household. They could not leave it at will, for they were usually apprentices or indentured servants, bound to serve for a period of several years, or else they were slaves. The master fed, clothed, and housed them, and supervised their behavior at all times. They could not even marry without his consent. A free craftsman sometimes worked for wages, and he might even live as a member of the family while he worked in it, but this was the exception. Most free crafts-men set up homes and businesses for themselves, with ser-vants of their own. In towns there were many such inde-pendent workmen—cobblers, coopers, cabinetmakers, silversmiths, tailors, tinsmiths, and many others—who in-cluded in their families a few servants to help them at their work. The townspeople furnished the customers to whom these craftsmen sold their wares, frequently in shops adjoining their homes. Thus a single family with the assistance of servants might perform the functions of factory and retail store together.

On the great plantations servants and slaves were even more important to the life of the family than they were in town. The plantation was a complete society in minia-ture, containing within itself almost all the trades and professions necessary for a civilized life. At Westover, on the James River, William Byrd ruled over what amounted to a small city. "I have a large Family of my own," he wrote to a friend in England, "and my Doors are open to Every Body, yet I have no Bills to pay, and half-a-Crown will rest undisturbed in my Pocket for many Moons together. Like one of the Patriarchs, I have my Flocks and my Herds, my Bond-men and Bond-women, and every Soart of Trade amongst my own Servants, so that I live in a kind of Independence on every one but Providence."

Byrd's way of life was not unusual in Virginia. Every plantation tended to become self-sufficient, growing to-bacco for trade with England and purchasing a few Eng-lish manufactures with the proceeds of the tobacco, but for the rest sustaining itself within its own bounds. The son of George Mason of Gunston Hall described how

A. L. Dementi

Rich plantations lined the banks of her rivers for a hundred miles into the interior.

This view of Westover, the home of William Byrd II, shows its command of the river.

The plantation was a complete society in miniature, containing within itself almost all the trades and professions necessary for a civilized life.

The blacksmith who operated a forge like this might be
either a hired servant or a slave specially
trained for the purpose.

the eighteenth-century planters lived in splendid independence:

It was very much the practise with gentlemen of landed and slave estates in the interior of Virginia, so to organize them as to have considerable resources within themselves; to employ and pay but few tradesmen and to buy little or none of the coarse stuffs and materials used by them, and this practise became stronger and more general during the long period of the Revolutionary War which in great measure cut off the means of supply from elsewhere. Thus my father had among his slaves carpenters, coopers, sawyers, blacksmiths, tanners, curriers, shoemakers, spinners, weavers and knitters, and even a distiller. His woods furnished timber and plank for the carpenters and coopers, and charcoal for the blacksmith; his cattle killed for his own consumption and for sale supplied skins for the tanners, curriers, and shoemakers, and his sheep gave wool and his fields produced cotton and flax for the weavers and spinners, and his orchards fruit for the distiller. His carpenters and sawyers built and kept in repair all the dwelling-houses, barns, stables, ploughs, harrows, gates &c., on the plantations and the outhouses at the home house. His coopers made the hogsheads the tobacco was prized in and the tight casks to hold the cider and other liquors. The tanners and curriers with the proper vats &c., tanned and dressed the skins as well for upper as for lower leather to the full amount of the consumption of the estate, and the shoemakers made them into shoes for the negroes. A professed shoemaker was hired for three or four months in the year to come and make up the shoes for the white part of the family. The blacksmiths did all the iron work required by the establishment, as making and repairing ploughs, harrows, teeth chains, bolts &c., &c. The spinners, weavers and knitters made all the coarse cloths and stockings used by the negroes, and some of finer texture worn by the white family, nearly all worn by the children of it. The distiller made every fall a good deal of apple, peach and persimmon brandy. The art of distilling from grain was not then among us, and but few public distilleries. All these operations were carried on at the home house, and their results distributed as occasion required to the different plantations. Moreover all the beeves and hogs for consumption or sale were driven up and slaughtered there at the proper seasons, and whatever was to be preserved was salted and packed away for after distribution.

Obviously the problem of servants in a family of this size was something beyond the experience of any head of a household in America today. The servants and slaves on a plantation were not there simply to do the dishes and sweep the floor: they corresponded rather to the men and machines that furnish our own complex society with all its worldly goods. They ranged from the tutor who instructed the children to the field hand who cut tobacco and the blacksmith who shod the horses. It is not surprising that the men and women who filled these different offices should have enjoyed different degrees of social prestige.

Probably the highest rank was accorded the tutor, particularly if he was a college-bred man. Fithian told his successor at Nomini Hall, John Peck, that the Virginians placed a high value on mental acquirements and that a graduate of Princeton though without any fortune was rated as high in the social scale as a man with an estate of £10,000. Fithian advised Peck to assume a position in the family "at a perfect equidistance between the father and the eldest Son." Peck was so successful in maintaining his dignity that he was able to marry one of the girls he was hired to tutor—and with her father's blessing. Even if he were an indentured servant, bound to serve his master for four years, the tutor was generally accepted in the family almost as a social equal. He had the use of his master's library; he dined with the family, and sometimes he even shared a room with one of the sons. Usually some servant or slave was assigned to take care of both his schoolroom and his bedroom. He might accompany the family to barbecues and balls and visits among the neighbors. When school was not in session, he was more like a guest than a servant.

Other servants who maintained a high social standing, though not as high as the tutor's, were those like the shoemaker at Gunston Hall, who worked for wages. This group usually included any overseers whom the planter might employ and any laborers skilled in trades with which the slaves or indentured servants on the plantation were not acquainted. These hired servants, as might be expected in a land where labor was scarce, had to be handled with care, lest they walk out and leave the master stranded with a job half done. They regarded themselves as superior to the other servants and expected the master to treat them accordingly. Once William Byrd offered his hired boatwright a breakfast of corn-bread, the usual food for servants on a plantation, instead of the wheat bread which the rest of the family ate. The boatwright rode off on his horse without a word and did not return to work that day. When William Daingerfield criticized an overseer for a fault, the man tossed in the air the keys of the buildings under his charge and likewise rode away.

Such independence constituted a special problem which can perhaps be understood sympathetically by anyone concerned with the management of labor. But catering to prima donnas was not the main servant problem in colonial Virginia. Wage earners at least work voluntarily, but most servants were unwilling members of the family in which they served. They had little or nothing to gain by their work, and the master could never have kept them in subjection without the assistance of the colonial government.

The indentured servants had at least exercised some measure of personal choice. These men and women, who had found no place on the social ladder in England or Europe, had come to America in order to take advantage of the opportunities of the new world. Without the money to pay their way across the ocean they had bartered four years or more of their lives in return for the privilege of spending two months on a ship making the voyage to America. The man who carried them over or paid their passage gained the title to their labor for a period of years and might sell that title as he chose. The importation of servants was actually a business in itself, in which a number of middlemen profited before the servant reached his final master. Sometimes dealers known as "soul-drivers" purchased whole shiploads of servants and drove them through the countryside, selling them like so many pots and pans to whoever would buy. More often a ship carrying servants would anchor off Leedstown or Yorktown, where a dealer would advertise the cargo and those who needed servants would come and purchase them. In any case, by the time a servant reached the home of the man with whom he would serve out his time, he was apt to be pretty thoroughly disgruntled. The value of his service for the time assigned was usually far higher than the price his master had paid, so that he owed no debt of gratitude. Certainly he would not be apt to exert himself strenuously where he would receive none of the profit of his labor.

The indentured servant, however, had more reason to be contented than most of his fellow workers. He may have signed his indenture without knowing exactly what he was getting in for, but unless he had been kidnapped by some unscrupulous ship captain, he came to America voluntarily, with the realization that for a period of years his time would belong to someone else. This advantage was not enjoyed by another class of English servants brought to Virginia in large numbers in the eighteenth century: the convicts. Criminals facing execution in England were sometimes given the alternative of transportation to the colonies with their labor to be sold for a period of seven or fourteen years depending on the gravity of the offence, partly as a punishment and partly in order to pay the costs of transportation. Convicts served Virginia masters in a variety of capacities. They were frequently highly skilled in industrial trades and furnished a valuable addition to the labor force of the colony. But as convicted felons they were not apt to have the best moral character, and they might even present a real danger to the family which harbored them. One smooth-tongued villain by the name of Anthony Richards persuaded his master, Robert Grier, to set him free. No sooner had Grier done so than Richards disappeared, along with Grier's horse, watch, silverware, gun, two beds, two tables, and—Mrs. Grier. Even after a convict had served out his time, he might do the family damage. He would have an intimate knowledge of the circumstances and habits of the household, knowledge which would make theft easy for him. Landon Carter attributed to an ex-servant the theft of a copper still that had required six men to carry when it was installed.

Both convicts and indentured servants continued to arrive in Virginia, sometimes hundreds in a single year, up to the time of the Revolution, but during the eighteenth century they were always a minority of the colony's labor force. Most of the work which made Virginia a pleasant place for some people to live in was done by slaves. And if it was a problem for the head of a family to keep his servants working efficiently, the problem with slaves was tenfold worse, for here were men and women who could never look forward to an end of their servitude. An indentured servant might be constrained to good behavior by fear of having the courts extend his period of service, as they would if he ran away or injured his master's interests in any way. For a slave there was no incentive to work except the lash.

It has been pointed out that slaves were fed and clothed by their master, that they never had to worry about unemployment or old age. In material comforts they were frequently better off than free workmen. If slaves had been cattle, these conditions would have been sufficient to bring contentment. But even cattle must be driven. Slavery was not a benevolent institution, and slaveowners themselves did not regard it as such. To be sure they had no desire to be cruel for cruelty's sake, nor did they have anything to gain by injuring slaves for whom they had paid good money. But slavery was designed to benefit the master alone, not the slave, and the slaveowners of colonial Virginia knew no other way to keep their slaves working than to beat them.

William Byrd, who was as cultivated and sophisticated a gentleman as Virginia produced in the eighteenth century, frequently recorded beating his slaves. One night in Williamsburg when he had stayed out late playing cards, he came back to his lodgings to find that his man had gone to bed and shut him out. "However," he says, "I called him and beat him for it." One day he beat the cook for not boiling the bacon long enough. On another day his wife "caused several of the people to be whipped for their laziness." On another he kicked one of the maids for lighting a candle before dark. Occasionally the slaves suffered simply because he and his wife had quarreled, as when he wrote, "My wife caused Prue to be whipped violently notwithstanding I desired not, which provoked me to have Anaka whipped likewise who had deserved it much more."

Byrd certainly did not consider himself a cruel man, nor did he have that reputation. These whippings were mere routine on a great plantation. The slaves doubtless suffered much more heavily at the hands of overseers, who had no proprietary interest in them, than they did from their owners. Fithian recorded with horror a formula described to him by an overseer for dealing with an unruly slave—a grisly business involving curry combs and salt. Such sadistic methods were doubtless frowned upon by decent slaveowners, yet the whipping of slaves to death was by no means unknown, and many planters practiced what appear to us to be rather barbarous punishments. Byrd evidently had some sort of a bridle that he made slaves wear as a punishment. Other masters fastened iron collars around the necks of rebellious slaves and even of servants. George Turburville chained his coachman to the chariot box, and John Randolph branded at least one of his slaves with the letters "I R" on both cheeks. There was certainly enough of this sort of thing going on in the Northern Neck when Fithian was there in 1774 to make the planters squirm uncomfortably when the local parson preached a sermon against the common practice of abusing slaves.

This abuse would not have been necessary if the slaves had worked for their masters contentedly, but the slaves demonstrated again and again that they were not contented. The new Negroes, as those who were brought from Africa were called, fought against their status chiefly by feigning stupidity. It came to be accepted that a new Negro was good for nothing until he had been subjected to a long training period. An English observer, by no means friendly to the institution of slavery, wrote: "To be sure, a *new Negro*, if he must be broke, either from Obstinacy, or, which I am more apt to suppose, from Greatness of Soul, will require more hard Discipline than a young Spaniel: You would really be surpriz'd at their Perserverance; let an hundred Men shew him how to hoe, or drive a Wheelbarrow, he'll still take the one by the Bottom, and the other by the Wheel; and they often die before they can be conquer'd."

It is very unlikely that the new Negroes were so stupid that they required long teaching to learn the use of the hoe, for the hoe was the principal instrument of cultivation in Africa. A new Negro must have been familiar with it before he arrived in Virginia. His feigned stupidity was doubtless a form of protest, a means of avoiding work.

Negroes born in Virginia often protested against their position by running away; every issue of the *Virginia Gazette* contained advertisements for runaways. Occasionally they hatched conspiracies to murder their masters; though no large-scale insurrection of slaves was accomplished in eighteenth-century Virginia, there were many small ones, and the planters lived in constant fear

In the evening they might gossip with neighbors or gather to dance and sing.

"The Old Plantation" was probably painted about 1800. Though it is thought to be from North Carolina, the buildings in the distance are reminiscent of Virginia architecture in the eighteenth century.

On most plantations the children, white and colored, played together.

Charles Calvert with a slave boy, painted in Maryland in 1761 by John Hesselius.

lest the enemy in their midst should join hands with the French and Indians who threatened from the outside.

The Virginia planters pondered often over the problem of slavery, and recognized it as an evil. It was probably no coincidence that a Virginian who himself held slaves gave classic statement to the doctrine of equality. When Jefferson wrote in the Declaration of Independence that all men are created equal, he realized that he and his neighbors were guilty of violating this principle. He and many other Virginians were convinced that slavery not only degraded the slave but brutalized the master. Yet neither Jefferson nor any other Virginian knew how to eradicate the evil. There was no way to abolish slavery without creating other evils which seemed equally undesirable. So much of a planter's capital was invested in slaves that, if he freed them, he would be obliged to abandon the standard of living which made him a planter. Worse still, a planter would not ordinarily have been in a position to give his slaves their freedom simply as a gesture of good will, for he was apt to be heavily indebted to a London merchant, and he felt the legal obligation to a creditor more strongly than the philanthropic one to his slaves. Sometimes a master did provide for manumission in his will, and in this way there grew up in Virginia a substantial class of free Negroes. But more often a man felt obliged to his children in death as he had to his creditors in life, and preferred to bequeath comfort to them rather than independence to his slaves. Morever, many believed already that the problem was one of race as well as of status and that two races could not exist in freedom side by side. Consequently Negro slaves continued to furnish the main labor force of Virginia, and the Virginians were obliged to make the best of it.

The best was none too good, even from the standpoint of the master, for labor performed unwillingly is not apt to be performed efficiently. From the standpoint of the slave, the best that could be expected was practically nothing. Yet there were gradations and distinctions which gave to some slaves a more bearable life than to others. These distinctions arose from the differing tasks assigned to the slaves. At the bottom of the pyramid stood the field hands, the unskilled laborers who hoed the weeds and cut the tobacco under the direction of an overseer. Both men and women were included in this group, which made up the majority of the slave population. On the larger plantations or on those managed exclusively by overseers, they had relatively little contact with their master. They were so many machines for the production of tobacco or wheat and did not form in any human sense a part of the plantation family, even though many masters did take pains to become acquainted with the field hands on their home plantation.

A step above the field hands in comfort and dignity were the skilled slave artisans who helped to make a plantation self-sufficient. These were men who had been born in the colony and instructed in youth by some craftsman employed on the plantation, either another slave or a white servant. Masters occasionally apprenticed promising slave boys to free artisans off the plantation. During the term of apprenticeship the boy would serve the master to whom he was apprenticed. When the term was up, he would return to his owner and practice his craft for his owner's benefit. These slaves were much more valuable than common field hands and were probably treated with more consideration as a result. A slave craftsman was in a better position than a field hand to exert pressure by the slowdown. If a field hand shirked, he could be detected and beaten, but it was more difficult to catch a blacksmith or a cooper or a shoemaker in the act. Even if it had been possible, as it patently was not, to have an overseer supervise each artisan, the skilled man could lower his rate of work without giving apparent notice of it in his activities. It must have been necessary therefore to conciliate the artisans by some kind of preferential treatment. They came in more direct and more frequent contact with their masters and the master took pains to build up good relations with them in so far as it was possible for good relations to exist between master and slave.

On a still higher level than the artisans stood the slaves who were employed as domestics within the mansion: the maids and boys who waited on table, cleaned the house, nursed the children, and attended to the personal needs of the master and mistress. It was this level of servitude which produced the most tolerable human relations between master and slave and which has frequently been idealized in nostalgic historical romances. Although it is apparent from William Byrd's diary that the domestic servants did not escape beatings, there is also evidence that many masters built up a genuine attachment to their domestic slaves, and that the slaves returned the sentiment. The strongest attachments were those formed between children and their nurses. Eliza Custis, when her mother remarried after the death of Eliza's father, seems to have transferred most of her affection to her grandmother, Martha Washington, and her nurse. She was heartbroken when the nurse was given to her younger brother and sister, who had been adopted by George Washington and had gone to live at Mount Vernon. Whenever Eliza visited Mount Vernon, she went for long walks with her old nurse. The affection was evidently returned, for the nurse wept when she left Eliza, and came back to care for the girl during a period of illness. From numerous letters one gets the impression that house slaves received many favors. A mistress would pass on to her maid a dress of which she had grown tired. A master would hand out small change from time to time, and visitors to the family would give tips when they left. When a master died, he might leave bequests to his house slaves, and many masters even bequeathed them their freedom.

The number of slaves who were able to find a satisfactory place in the white man's society as domestics was necessarily small. Most slaves were excluded from the intimacy of the family and had to find their human relationships entirely with each other. Under the conditions imposed by their status this was no easy task. They were not free agents and could not readily form attachments or societies after the patterns offered by the white man. In the white man's world they were so many tools, and were obliged to spend most of their waking lives doing someone else's bidding. At the same time they were cut off from the habits, the customs, and the conventions which had guided their free ancestors. They were a people without a country and all the relations they could establish with each other were tenuous and temporary, mere threads which their masters might cut at any time. Doubtless many of the African habits did survive even under these conditions, but the slave's adjustment to life was not easy.

It might be argued that there was little adjustment for most slaves, because most of them were born into slavery. Although importation of slaves continued with few interruptions throughout the eighteenth century, there were many slaves in Virginia by the middle of the century who had been born there and who therefore had to make no adjustment from an African past to an American present. Yet those who were born in the colony had another adjustment to make which was at least as difficult, for slave children had open to them in childhood a freedom which they could never enjoy as adults. On most plantations the children, white and colored, played together, and children are great levelers, so far as the distinctions established by adults are concerned. Many slaves must have been able to remember defeating their masters in the various matches and games that children play together. Only gradually, as they grew up, were the white children withdrawn from the companionship of the black, and sometimes they became masters with as great reluctance as their colored friends became slaves. One of the most appealing children in history is Bob Carter, who was inordinately fond of horses and hunting and had little use for the social conventions upon which his elders set such store. He preferred the company of those who liked the things that he liked, and he did not stop to ask his friends for their pedigrees. One night at Nomini Hall when Bob was fourteen, Fithian observed an episode which illustrates how a genuine comradeship might exist between the children and slaves of a plantation:

There came in about eight o-Clock a man very drunk, and grew exceeding noisy and troublesome, and as the Evening was cold and stormy Mr Carter thought it improper to send him away; he was therefore ordered into the Kitchen, to stay the Night: Him Bob soon after persuaded to the School-house; I soon heard from my Room the noise and guesed immediately the Cause. I waited however 'til half after ten, when all seemed silent; I then took a candle and went into the School-Room, And before the Fire Bob had brought a matt, and Several Blankets, and was himself in a sound sleep covered with the Blankets on the same Matt between the drunken Man, and a Negro Fellow, his Papas Postilion! I mention this as one Example among a thousand to shew the very particular Taste of this Boy!

This sort of companionship could not go on indefinitely. Sooner or later the easy intimacy would give way, and a barrier would rise between the children who lived in the "great house" and those who lived in the quarters. The transformation must have made slavery even harder to bear than it would have been if slave children had been entirely excluded from the friendship of free children from the start. But human nature has an unpredictable resiliency, and slaves did manage to live a life of their own within the limits prescribed for them.

Those limits were close, but not so close as to preclude entirely the possibility of a private life. The slave was wakened before dawn and worked for his master until nearly sundown. At night he would doubtless be tired from the long day's work, but many observers noticed that the slave hoarded his energy during the day in order to save as much as possible for the nights. Though the owner might try to have all his slaves asleep at an early hour in order that they might be fresh for the next day's work, he did not expect them to work at night, and he could not effectively keep them from play when darkness fell. As soon as the day was over the slave quarters came to life for a few brief crowded hours of conversation and music and dancing. Sometimes the slaves of neighboring plantations would meet together for a celebration under the cover of darkness, with rum and brandy pilfered from the master's cellar. The next morning there would doubtless be sore backs when the slaves appeared for work still dizzy from the night's revels, but for a time, at least, they would have lived like other men.

Besides the nights, slaves had Sundays to themselves. There were also holidays on Shrove Tuesday, Good Friday, Christmas, and Easter, and sometimes on the king's and queen's birthdays. During all these holidays which amounted to some sixty days out of the year, the slaves were somewhat their own masters. They could not leave the plantation without their owner's written permission, but their time was their own and they could use it as they saw fit. Many took up the white man's religion and attended church or even held their own meetings for worship. Others arranged cockfights, and all took part in music and dancing. Negroes quickly learned to play the white man's musical instruments, particularly the violin, and frequently were called upon to perform at the balls and entertainments given by their masters. They were also fond of rum and brandy and probably got drunk as often as they could find the means. William Byrd, visiting Governor Spotswood on February 7, 1711, found all the servants tipsy. "The Governor had made a bargain with his servants that if they would forbear to drink upon the Queen's birthday, they might be drunk this day. They observed their contract and did their business very well and got very drunk today, in such a manner that Mrs. Russell's maid was forced to lay the cloth, but the cook in that condition made a shift to send in a pretty little dinner."

But drinking and dancing were not enough to satisfy all the emotional needs of men and women who spent most of their time in forced labor. It might be supposed that the removal of the restraints imposed by tribal customs would have resulted in sexual promiscuity among the slaves. In Africa the general run of Negro families had probably been monogamous, but polygamy was not illegal. Important men who were wealthy enough to support more than one wife frequently had several. Under conditions of slavery, where the master supported both women and children, the economic pressure toward monogamy was removed. Furthermore the masters had an economic interest in seeing the slaves reproduce themselves, and some were ready even to encourage promiscuity to promote this interest. With conditions so favorable there was doubtless a good deal of sexual license, and yet the need of enduring marital union asserted itself. Although slaves were never married in any formal ceremony, it was quite usual for couples to consider themselves as husband and wife and to remain faithful to one another even under the most trying conditions. Sometimes they belonged to different masters, and even if they lived on the same plantation, there was no guarantee they would not be separated by the sale of one or the other to a new master. That many husbands remained faithful to their wives in these circumstances is evident from the number of advertisements which state that a runaway slave had probably gone to visit his wife at a distant plantation.

Not only did slaves establish stable marriages, but they even were able to set up families among themselves. In most societies the family represents the division of labor in its simplest form, with the father earning a living and the mother looking after the household. Where both father and mother were required to work and daily bread was provided by the master, this primary economic motive for the establishment of family life was removed. The pattern of life in a slave family was accordingly a good deal different from that of other families in the eighteenth century, though curiously enough not so different from that of a modern family. Slave families usually lived in cabins provided by their master and ate food provided by their master. Rarely were they housed in barracks or fed in a common mess hall. On most plantations each family had a cabin to itself, where the wife prepared the food for the whole family. Since both mother and father must work all day, the mother could not stay home to look after the household and tend to the children. When she and her husband went off to field or workshop after an early breakfast of corn bread, she would leave her children at a common nursery where some older woman looked after the children of all the slaves—much as a modern working mother leaves her small child at nursery school.

In the evening after a hard day's work the family would gather again in the cabin to have their supper, after which they might gossip with the neighbors or gather to dance and sing or play some eighteenth-century game. On Sundays the family might behave very much like a free family, for then the mother and father might be busy cultivating small plots of ground assigned to them by the master for their own personal use. Though the master provided food, he did not always provide enough to form a satisfactory diet for men and women who did manual work all day. He therefore allowed his slaves to fill out their supply by working Sundays on a half acre or so of land.

The slave's garden not only helped to give him enough to eat, but also enabled him to win a small measure of economic independence. Often he could produce enough by his Sunday labors so that he had a surplus to sell at the market. In fact slaves were such successful farmers in their small gardens that merchants set up stores at crossroads in Virginia for the sale of their produce. These merchants doubtless engaged in other types of trade as well, but that which they carried on with slaves certainly formed a substantial part of their business.

The existence of such merchants and the recognized right of slave families to earn money from their own plots of land gave the slaves a chance to expand their assets by illegal methods. It was generally forbidden for them to grow tobacco or wheat on their plots, since these were the staple products of the plantation, and it was feared the slaves might be tempted to steal from the main crop in order to add to their own. But every plantation had also its own vegetable garden and its own chicken coop, and it was not difficult for a slave to steal from these in order to add to the produce that he brought to market. The crossroads merchants were known to ask few questions about where the goods they purchased came from. When a Negro brought in large quantities of any product, the merchant would know that it had been stolen, but for that very reason he would be able to purchase it at less than the going price, and many merchants made good bargains in this way.

It was very difficult for a planter to obtain a conviction against a merchant whom he suspected of receiving stolen goods. Though he might obtain confessions from his own slaves, he would not be able to use this evidence in court, because Virginia courts did not admit the testimony of slaves. This difficulty is well illustrated by an advertisement that appeared in the *Virginia Gazette*:

Williamsburg June 20, 1751

Whereas some Person hath enticed a young Negroe Girl of mine, to steal curled Hair, and other Materials for Chairs from me, and sell it them; and as her Evidence against them is of no Use, I do hereby offer a Reward of Twenty Pistoles, for the Discovery of the said Person, to be paid, immediately, on their Conviction.

Thus the slave gained an ironic advantage by the very disabilities which his masters had placed upon him. And though there were heavy penalties against theft, one may be sure that a slave felt very little compunction about stealing from a man who had already in a sense stolen everything from him.

Slaves not only stole property but whenever the opportunity offered they stole time as well. It was so common for slaves to run away for a few days' vacation that advertisements for them were seldom inserted in the papers until they had been gone for several weeks. A slave engaged in one of these temporary escapes might very well find an opportunity for a more permanent vacation from his master. Labor, especially skilled labor, was scarce in Virginia, and a slave might be able to make a bargain to work for some white craftsman at less than the standard wages, in return for concealment from his owner. Thus one master advertised a runaway slave who was "a very good blacksmith, and, as supposed, is harboured by some white man of that trade."

If a slave succeeded in reaching a remote region like the Carolina frontier, he might even pass for a freedman and live unmolested for the rest of his life. William Byrd, while on an expedition to survey the border between

Virginia and North Carolina in 1728, came across a family of mulattoes "that call'd themselves free, tho' by the Shyness of the Master of the House, who took care to keep least in Sight, their Freedom seem'd a little Doubtful. It is certain many Slaves Shelter themselves in this Obscure Part of the World, nor will any of their righteous Neighbours discover them. On the Contrary, they find their Account in Settling such Fugitives on some out-of-the-way-corner of their Land, to raise Stocks for a mean and inconsiderable Share, well knowing their Condition makes it necessary for them to Submit to any Terms."

However harsh the terms imposed on these first "share-croppers," it is evident that they preferred such an existence to the slave quarters of a plantation. By living successfully in the precarious freedom of the frontier, they demonstrated conclusively their ability to share a place in the white man's world.

4

HOUSES AND HOLIDAYS

The houses of eighteenth-century Virginia, many of which still stand, are a revealing record of the families which lived in them. A simple frontier farmer, living from the land but not producing much surplus to bring to market, needed a minimum of space under cover. He had no great crop to store, and he was ordinarily contented to live with his family in a one-room cabin with not much more than a table, a couple of chairs, and a bed for furniture. Sometimes there was not even a bed, and the whole family, as William Byrd put it, "pigg'd lovingly together" on the floor. Such squalor was common in the region of the Carolina frontier. In the Valley, the homes of industrious Pennsylvania German farmers were more shipshape. Here the family might live in fairly cramped quarters, but there were always surplus crops, and barns to hold them. In fact it was observed that the barns in the Valley were larger than the houses.

The farms in the Piedmont and Tidewater area showed a much greater prosperity, with larger dwelling houses and more numerous dependent buildings. A typical large farm was advertised for sale in the *Virginia Gazette* of December 4, 1766. It was located in Hanover County on the Little River, and contained 453 acres, with these following buildings: "a new dwelling-house 42 by 18, with four fireplaces, and two brick cellars, store, kitchen, smoke-house, dairy underpinned with brick, and a new barn 44 by 32, all covered with heart shingles, also another barn 32 by 16, both ten feet pitch, three good apple orchards, with sundry other buildings too tedious to mention." This was actually large enough to be called a plantation, but not the kind of plantation for which Virginia in the eighteenth century has become famous. That would have been dominated by a great mansion house, much larger than the other buildings and located in such a way as to be the center of interest in the congregation of buildings which surrounded it.

The mansion at Nomini Hall was 76 feet long by 44 feet wide and two stories high, the lower story 17 feet and the upper 12 feet. At a distance of one hundred yards from each corner of the mansion stood four buildings, each of them 45 feet long, 27 feet wide, and a story and a half high: the schoolhouse, the laundry, the stable, and the coach house. Together these four buildings formed a square with the mansion house in the center. On one side of the mansion, and within the triangle which it formed with two of the corner houses, stood a row of minor buildings: the kitchen, the bakehouse, the dairy, the storehouse, and numerous smaller buildings, which Fithian apparently found too "tedious" to mention. On the other side of the mansion, beginning outside the square formed by the four corner houses, stood two rows of poplars, about three hundred yards in length, leading to the Richmond road and forming an avenue about fifty feet wide in which the Hall was magnificently framed at the end. Though there is no record of where the slave quarters were located, they were probably remote from the central area, and perhaps hidden from it by plantings.

The symmetry of the arrangement at Nomini Hall was typical. The great house of a plantation usually formed the focal point of a pattern, dominating its environs as the gentleman who lived in it dominated his family. The building itself was designed to show off the owner's position in society and his gracious manner of living. It announced to the world that he was a gentleman. The formal lines of both house and gardens displayed a reserved good taste, none of the showiness of the parvenu, but simple elegance of the kind that cultivated gentlemen always cherish. The elegance was not marred by the intrusion of homely utilitarian functions. The whole interior of the house was devoted to rooms where the gentleman and his family and guests might engage in the pursuits that were proper to people of their station. To be sure the upstairs was usually given to bedrooms, but even sleep could be dignified in the elaborate bedsteads of the eighteenth century.

On the first floor one room would be a dining room. There might be, as at Nomini Hall, a separate dining room for the children, so that meals could be enjoyed in peace by adults and children alike. Dining was a fine art in Virginia, and the planters took great pride in setting their tables with more food than anyone could eat. Fruits and vegetables of every kind appeared on the table at a single meal, along with several different meats. The dining room was a place to display one's hospitality and to enjoy fine conversation. Dinner, which came at two or three in the afternoon, was a ceremony not to be neglected by any member of the family, as Fithian discovered when he omitted it once. On June 15, 1774 he wrote in his journal, "I took a whim in my head and would not go to Dinner. My Head was not dress'd, and I was too lazy to change my clothes—Mrs. Carter, however, in the evening lash'd me severely. I told her I was engaged in reading a pleasant Novel.—That I was not perfectly well—But she would not hear none, and said I was rude, and censurable."

The business of preparing food, on the other hand, was no pastime for a lady or gentleman, even though the lady of the house might sometimes have to engage in it. The kitchen therefore was not a part of the house but a separate building, from which servants or slaves bore the food in covered dishes to the dining hall. Thus the aroma of cooking was excluded from the mansion along with the excessive heat of the kitchen fire.

An important room in every well-equipped plantation house was the library or study: Virginia gentlemen frequently had extensive collections of books which they obtained from London booksellers through their correspondents there. William Byrd spent a portion of every day reading from English, Greek, Hebrew, or Latin authors in his library and was always annoyed when hospitality or business interfered with this practice. Whether many planters were as assiduous readers as Byrd is perhaps questionable. It almost goes without saying that women did not read or write extensively. Their literary education generally ceased before they could become seriously interested in literature, and society frowned on a bookish woman. The library was a man's room, and Byrd even recorded in his diary once that he refused to allow his wife to borrow a book!

On some plantations there might be a game room with

Another grand occasion was the hunt.
"The End of the Hunt." From the collection of American
primitive paintings given by Edgar William and Bernice
Chrysler Garbisch, National Gallery of Art.

Thomas L. Williams

Families arrived some time before the service began and chatted outside until the minister called them in.
Bruton Parish Church, Williamsburg, Virginia.

a billiard table and tables for playing cards. Byrd had a billiard table at Westover and used it frequently, sometimes with visitors, sometimes with his wife, for billiards was considered a proper enough pastime for ladies in the eighteenth century. Byrd also played cards with his wife and noted once that he provoked her by cheating. Probably all these games were played for money, for Virginians were fond of gambling. Even the children gambled. Little Sally Fairfax recorded winning ten shillings from a Mr. William Payne at checks, a game played with peach stones. It also seems likely that she won regularly from her mother, for according to one entry in her diary, "on thursday, the 16th of Jan. [1772] there came a woman and a girl and mama bought 3 old hens from them, and gave them to me, which reduced her debt she owed me, which was 5 and nine pence to three and ninepence, which she now owes me, and she owes me fiveteen pence about Nancy Perey's ribon which she never paid."

The largest and probably most important room in a great mansion was the ballroom. The one at Nomini Hall was thirty feet long, and others were even larger. This room might be used for any reception or entertainment. It was also the headquarters for the dancing school when the traveling dancing master came to instruct the young ladies and gentlemen of the neighborhood. At Nomini Hall, when the dancing school had closed and the pupils had been dismissed, the rest of the family, who had been present as spectators, stayed on for parlor games: ". . . at the proposal of several," wrote Fithian, "(with Mr Carters approbation) we played *Button*, to get Pauns for Redemption; here I could join with them, and indeed it was carried on with sprightliness, and Decency; in the course of redeeming my Pauns, I had several Kisses of the

Ladies! . . . So soon as we rose from supper, the Company form'd into a semicircle round the fire, and Mr Lee, by the voice of the Company was chosen *Pope*, and Mr Carter, Mr Christian, Mrs *Carter*, Mrs *Lee*, and the rest of the company were appointed Friars, in the Play call'd 'break the Popes neck'—Here we had great diversion in the respective Judgments upon offenders, but we were all dimiss'd by ten, and retired to our several rooms."

The time when the ballroom really dominated the scene was when the planter gave his annual or semi-annual ball. This might be an affair lasting for two or three days during which the liquor flowed freely and lavish tables were set every day. Those who did not care to dance might sit all night at card tables. During the day both ladies and gentlemen would catch a wink of sleep, those who lived near by at their own homes, those who came from a distance in rooms provided by the host. In the afternoon and evening after hours of elaborate dressing and primping, both ladies and gentlemen would return to the ball, and the same the next day and night, until everyone was exhausted. Whole families came by coach for the festivities. When Sally Fairfax's father gave a ball at Christmastime, one mother even "brought her sucking child with her." Philip Fithian has left the best picture of a Virginia ball—although the occasion was for him a painful one—in his journal of 1774.

We set away from Mr Carters at two; Mrs *Carter* & the young Ladies in the Chariot, Mrs Lane in a Chair, & myself on Horseback—As soon as I had handed the Ladies out, I was saluted by Parson *Smith;* I was introduced into a small Room where a number of Gentlemen were playing Cards, (the first game I have seen since I left Home) to lay off my Boots Riding-Coat &c—Next I was directed into the Dining-

Room to see Young Mr *Lee;* He introduced me to his Father—With them I conversed til Dinner, which came in at half after four. The Ladies dined first, when some Good order was preserved; when they rose, each nimblest Fellow dined first—The Dinner was as elegant as could be well expected when so great an Assembly were to be kept for so long a time.—For Drink, there was several sorts of Wine, good Lemon Punch, Toddy, Cyder, Porter &c.—About Seven the Ladies & Gentlemen begun to dance in the Ball-Room—first Minuets one Round; Second Giggs; third Reels; And last of All Country-Dances; tho' they struck several Marches occasionally—The Music was a French-Horn and two Violins—The Ladies were Dressed Gay, and splendid, & when dancing, their Silks & Brocades rustled and trailed behind them!—But all did not join in the Dance for there were parties in Rooms made up, some at Cards; some drinking for Pleasure; some toasting the Sons of america; some singing "Liberty Songs" as they call'd them, in which six, eight, ten or more would put their Heads near together and roar, & for the most part as unharmonious as an affronted— Among the first of these Vociferators was a young Scotch-Man, Mr *Jack Cunningham;* he was nimis bibendo appotus; noisy, droll, waggish, yet civil in his way & wholly inoffensive—I was solicited to dance by several, Captain Chelton, Colonel Lee, Harry Lee, and others; But George Lee, with great Rudeness as tho' half drunk, asked me why I would come to the Ball & neither dance nor play Cards? I answered him shortly, (for his Impudence moved my resentment) that my Invitation to the Ball would Justify my Presence; & that he was ill qualified to direct my Behaviour who made so indifferent a Figure himself—Parson Smiths, & Parson Gibberns Wives danced, but I saw neither of the Clergymen either dance or game—At Eleven Mrs Carter call'd upon me to go, I listned with gladness to the summons & with Mrs Lane in the Chariot we rode Home, the Evening sharp and cold!—I handed the Ladies out, waited on them to a warm Fire, then ran over to my own Room, which was warm and had a good Fire; oh how welcome! Better this than to

be at the Ball in some corner nodding, and awaked now &
then with a midnight Yell!

Some of the most elegant balls in Virginia were held
in Williamsburg while the Assembly was in session. Here
the governor gave an extremely lavish entertainment on
the king's birthday. And there were even professional
entertainers who gave weekly balls with admission by
ticket. English travelers found the Virginians immod-
erately fond of dancing. Andrew Burnaby, who visited
the colony in 1760, described the dances which were
usually performed at the fashionable balls. To begin
with there were minuets and country dances. Then, "Towards the close of an evening, when the company are
pretty well tired with country dances, it is usual to dance
jigs; a practice originally borrowed, I am informed, from
the negroes. These dances are without method or regularity: a gentleman and lady stand up, and dance about
the room, one of them retiring, the other pursuing, then
perhaps meeting, in an irregular fantastical manner. After
some time, another lady gets up, and then the first lady
must sit down, she being, as they term it, cut out: the
second lady acts the same part which the first did, till
somebody cuts her out. The gentlemen perform in the
same manner."

The Virginians' passion for dancing was not confined
to the wealthy families of the Tidewater and Piedmont.
Even in the back country dancing was the principal
form of entertainment. We have already noticed the
dancing which followed frontier weddings. The sister of
an officer in Braddock's army described a ball at Frederick Town, Maryland attended by what seemed to her
an uncouth crowd of people. "The Ladys danced without

Stays or Hoops, and it ended with a jig from each Lady." The absence of stays and hoops must have given the ball at Frederick Town a much different appearance from those held in the mansions of the Tidewater, where the ladies were laced within an inch of their lives.

The presence of the ballroom in a Virginia mansion was a symbol of the planter's hospitality, for a ball was not something to be enjoyed alone; it was an entertainment in which the planter did everything he could to give his friends and neighbors a good time. The families living on plantations in eighteenth-century Virginia were almost self-sufficient economically, and therefore had little occasion to see their neighbors on business, but they took pains to meet very often simply in order to enjoy each other's company. The annual ball was only the most formal occasion upon which they entertained each other. Another grand event was the hunt, a popular recreation with many planters, and one which could be enjoyed in company. There were many lesser occasions which gave an excuse for a get-together. When a baby was born, the christening was usually performed at home and all the neighbors attended. Church itself was as much an opportunity for conversation as a ceremony of worship. Families arrived some time before the service began and chatted outside until the minister called them in. After the service was finished they gossiped outside for another half an hour or more and concluded by inviting one another home to dinner.

The pervasive religious atmosphere of New England was generally lacking in Virginia. In the Valley, German Lutherans and Scotch-Irish Presbyterians took an interest in religion that resembled that of the New Englanders, but in the Tidewater and Piedmont the publicly supported Anglican Church fell very much under the secular influence of its wealthier members. Northern visitors were sometimes shocked to see clergymen dancing and gaming with their parishioners. The Anglican Church was not widely affected by the religious revivals which shook other colonial churches in the eighteenth century, and the few non-Anglican ministers who labored in eastern Virginia found that family prayers were neglected and the Sabbath violated regularly. Even those Anglican ministers who took their work seriously wielded less influence than did their colleagues in the North. The planters of Virginia were a sophisticated group of men, and while they remained faithful members of the established church, they were apt to take their religious beliefs pretty much for granted and to concentrate their attention on living gracefully.

When the weather was mild, the planters enjoyed picnicking on a grand scale. In the early years families used to gather at some point by the river for a "fish-feast" or a barbecue, each family bringing its own food. As time wore on and the planters grew more and more opulent, it became customary for them to treat each other to these affairs. Landon Carter wrote in his diary that he thought the old way preferable. "I confess," he said, "I like to meet my friends now and then, but certainly the old plan of every family carrying its own dish was both cheaper and better, because then nobody intruded, but now every one comes in and raises the club, and really many do so only for the sake of getting a good dinner and a belly full of drink."

Landon Carter was an eccentric. Other Virginians found no fault in expensive entertainments whether they could afford them or not. On most Virginia plantations there was no such thing as an intruder. The doors were open to anyone who passed, friend or stranger. Everyone was entertained according to his rank, the gentleman in the manor house, the humble wayfarer by the kitchen fire. As early as 1702, Francis Louis Michel, a Swiss traveling through the country, discovered the fabulous Virginia hospitality. "It is possible," he wrote, "to travel through the whole country without money, except when ferrying across a river. . . . Even if one is willing to pay, they do not accept anything, but they are rather angry, asking, whether one did not know the custom of the country. At first we were too modest to go into the houses to ask for food and lodging, which the people often recognized, and they admonished us not to be bashful, as this was the custom of rich and poor."

Virginians enjoyed hospitality so much that they spent a great deal of time simply in visiting one another, quite apart from the large-scale get-togethers at barbecues, balls, and fish-feasts. Usually the visit was only a morning or afternoon call. Virginians liked to ride, and often they would make a visit to a neighboring plantation the excuse for a canter. Sometimes they made longer visits to friends and relations who lived at some distance. The wealthier families were almost all related in some way by blood or marriage, and it was thought proper to keep in communication with all one's aunts, uncles, and cousins by visiting them. Young people in particular, who were not yet troubled with the responsibilities of running a plantation or keeping a house in order, might go off on a round of visits lasting for several weeks. One of the most delightful documents that has survived from colonial Virginia is the journal of a young lady who with several companions made a tour of her friends' homes in 1782, staying a few days with each, gossiping, flirting, and dancing. The most entertaining visit was that which she paid to the Washingtons (relatives of the General), who were fond of practical jokes. "About sunset," she writes, "Nancy, Milly, and myself took a walk in the Garden (it is a most butifull place.) We were mighty busy cutting thistles to try our sweethearts, when Mr. Washington caught us; and you can't conceive how he plagued us—chased us all over the Garden, and was quite impertinent." After they went to bed, the girls got hungry and decided to raid the larder: "We took it into our heads to want to eat; well, we had a large dish of bacon and beaf; after that, a bowl of Sago cream; and after that, an apple pye. While we were eating the apple pye in bed —God bless you, making a great noise—in came Mr. Washington, dressed in Hannah's short gown and petticoat, and seazed me and kissed me twenty times, in spite of all the resistance I could make; and then Cousin Molly. Hannah soon follow'd dress'd in his Coat. They joined in eating the apple pye, and then went out. After this we took it into our heads to want to eat oysters. We got up, put on our rappers, and went down in the Seller to get them: do you think Mr. Washington did not follow us and scear us just to death. We went up tho, and eat our oysters. We slept in the old Lady's room too, and she sat laughing fit to kill herself at us."

So respectable was it to visit one's friends for weeks at a time that needy gentlemen occasionally took advantage of this hospitality to save their own pocketbooks. While Fithian was at Nomini Hall the Carters received without apparent irritation a visit from a man who made a habit of living off his friends. Fithian wrote on January 21, 1774, "To Day about twelve came to Mr *Carters* Captain *John Lee*, a Gentleman who seems to copy the Character of *Addisons Will Wimble*. When I was on my way to this place I saw him up in the country at Stafford; he was then just sallying out on his Winters Visit, and has got now so far as here, he stays, as I am told about eight, or ten Weeks in the year at his own House, the remaining part he lives with his waiting Man on his Friends.—"

The pattern of social life established by the wealthy planters was copied, so far as possible, by the small number of merchants and professional men who lived in Williamsburg, Fredericksburg, Norfolk, and the few other towns of colonial Virginia. Life in town was on a smaller scale, but here too houses were built with a view to dignified living. Kitchens and other utility rooms were separated from the main house wherever the owner could afford it. The better houses in town, like the manor houses of the plantations, tell much about the people who lived in them. But the dwellings of the lower-class families, whether in town or country, are less revealing. The one-room or two-room cabin of the farmer conveys little about its inhabitants beyond the fact that they had no comfort or privacy.

This much, however, it says eloquently. The kind of life which a family can live in one room is vastly different from the kind which can be lived in a mansion. When everyone must eat and sleep in the same room, there will not be much space for delicacy. In the winter it was even necessary to make a virtue of the cramped quarters: everyone huddled together in the same bed to keep warm, including visitors who happened to pass by and whom the family would no more turn away than would the wealthiest planter. Under these circumstances formality must have been at a minimum, and children must have become acquainted with the facts of life at an early age.

Such families must have spent most of their time working in the fields and a good share of the remainder of it in spinning and weaving to keep themselves clothed. We know that a family of four, with no servants, could turn out as much as thirty-nine yards of cloth and four pairs of stockings in a single year. In order to keep up that rate, both mother and children must have had to stick to the spinning wheel and the loom pretty constantly. But some jobs could furnish the excuse for a community frolic. Even the simplest of farm families enjoyed husking bees, quilting bees, house-raisings, and harvestings. Francis Louis Michel left an account of a harvesting celebration in 1702:

The custom of the country, when the harvest is to be gathered in, is to prepare a dinner, to which the neighbors are invited, and for which two men have sufficient work to do. There are often from thirty to fifty persons cutting grain, so that frequently they have work for only two hours. This is one of the principal festivals or times of rejoicing. When I was unable to travel at one time, because of the rain, I stayed at a house, where they intended to cut wheat that day. When everything was ready to receive the guests at noon, it looked in the morning as if the weather was going to be favorable. Ten persons had already arrived, when the weather changed and turned into a violent rain, so that hope to harvest in a few days came to nothing. Fresh meat cannot be kept in summer longer than twenty-four hours, hence the good people were compelled . . . to entertain us, which lasted for a day and a half.

All segments of the population, in town and country alike, attended horse races and cockfights. The rich, of course, furnished the horses and cocks and won or lost most heavily in the betting, but these events not only provided exciting spectacles for the whole community but furnished a continuing topic of conversation and interest. Another sort of contest that always drew a crowd was a wrestling match, whether spontaneous or prearranged. Fighting in Virginia was catch as catch can, and must have been somewhat gruesome to watch. Men who enjoyed fighting or who anticipated getting into a fight used to let their fingernails grow long in order to have a better chance at the other fellow's eyes!

Men of all classes found relaxation in the evening by visiting the nearest tavern. A townsman could choose from a number of these, and even the farmer was apt to be within reach of at least one crossroads tavern where he could drink and gossip and gamble with his neighbors. According to a clergyman's complaint printed in the *Virginia Gazette* in 1751, taverns had been perverted from their original purpose of supporting travelers and had "become the common Receptacle, and Rendezvous of the very Dreggs of the People; even of the most lazy and dissolute that are to be found in their respective Neighbourhoods, where not only Time and Money are, vainly and unprofitably, squandered away, but (what is yet worse) where prohibited and unlawful Games, Sports, and Pastimes are used, followed, and practised, almost without any Intermission; namely Cards, Dice, Horse-racing, and Cock-fighting, together with Vices and Enormities of every other Kind."

An entertainment which all the family could enjoy was the annual fair held in the different counties, such as the one established in Hanover County in 1737. The celebration included a handsome dinner to the accompaniment of music by drums, trumpets, and oboes, followed by the drinking of healths to their majesties and the governor. Diversion was to be provided by a great variety of contests: a horse race for a purse of five pounds, a hat worth twenty shillings to be cudgeled for, a violin to be played for by twenty fiddlers (after the prize was awarded all the fiddlers were "to play together, and each a different Tune; and to be treated by the Company"). A quire of ballads was to be sung for, and all of the songsters were to be given "Liquor sufficient to clear their Wind-Pipes." A pair of silver buckles was to be wrestled for, a pair of handsome shoes to be danced for, and finally "a Pair of handsome Silk Stockings of One Pistole Value, [to] be given to the handsomest young Country Maid that appears in the Field: With many other Whimsical and Comical Diversions, too tedious to mention here." Similar fairs were established at the principal town in other counties, where people would gather once a year from the surrounding country to enjoy the same kind of diversions.

Sometimes a special event called for a holiday in which everyone could take part. One such occasion widely celebrated in Virginia was the triumph of the king's forces over the Jacobite rebels at Culloden Moor. The festivities at Norfolk upon receipt of the news were typical. An elaborate parade was arranged, described in the newspapers as follows:

1st. Three Drummers, 2d. a Piper, 3d. Three Violins, 4th. Six Men with long white Rods, with Slips of Paper like Sashes over their Shoulders, and different Mottoes wrote on them in Capital Letters, as, Liberty and Property, and no Pretender. No Pretender. No Wooden Shoes, &c. &c. 5th. a Man in Women's Cloaths, dress'd like a Nurse, carrying a Warming-pan, with a Child peeping out of it. 6th. The Pretender in his Two-arm'd Chair, drawn in a Cart. 7th. Six Men, two and two, with drawn Cutlasses, and lastly, a vast Crowd of People of the Town and Country, who thus marched in Procession thro' all the Streets, 'till they came (about One o'Clock) to the Center of the Three main Streets, where a Gibbet being erected for the Purpose, the Cart was drawn under it, and his Pretendership was immediately exalted, to the general View and Satisfaction of the Spectators. Liquor was provided for the better Sort; and the Populace had great Plenty in Casks standing with one Head out. On drinking the Health of his Majesty King *George* II, a Royal Salute was made of 21 Guns planted in two different Places; which was answered by a Number of others from the Vessels in the Harbour. Then followed other loyal Healths, as, the Royal Family, His Royal Highness the Duke, the Governor and *Virginia*, Success to his Majesty's Arms, &c. each Health being proclaimed by the Guns at the two different Parts of the Town, and Vessels in the Harbour. Thus the Gentlemen continued at the Court-house, 'til the Evening; when the Windows were all over the Town beautifully illuminated. Then a large Bonfire was kindled round the Gibbet, and in a few Minutes the Effigie dropt into the Flames; then there was another Royal Salute, accompany'd with loud Huzza's, and Acclamations of Joy. To conclude, that the Ladies might also partake of the Rejoicings on this extraordinary Occasion, the Gentlemen entertained them with a Ball; and the Evening concluded with innocent Mirth and unaffected Joy, becoming a People Loyal to their King, and zealous for their Country's Good.

Those families who were fortunate enough to live in or near a town like Fredericksburg or Williamsburg, and those who were wealthy enough to come to Williamsburg for the sitting of the Assembly, could enjoy a variety of entertainment. During most of the year Williamsburg was a sleepy college town, but during "Publick Times" when the Assembly was in session, Williamsburg enjoyed social attractions of every kind.

Besides balls and fairs, there was a theatre where companies of actors came and performed both comedies and tragedies. The inhabitants of Williamsburg in the four decades preceding the Revolution were able to see *The Merchant of Venice*, *The Anatomist*, *The Constant Couple*, *Richard III*, *The Busy-Body*, *The Recruiting Officer*, *The Beaux' Strategem*, *The Beggar's Opera*, Addison's *Cato*, and probably many others. Besides regular plays there was sometimes theatrical dancing. In 1751 a company performed "A Grand Tragic Dance, compos'd by Monsieur *Denoier*, call'd the Royal Captive, after the *Turkish* Manner, as perform'd at His Majesty's Opera House, in the Hay-Market." The following year the program included a dance called "the Drunken Peasant." In 1766 in Fredericksburg there was a concert played by three violins, two flutes, a oboe, a horn, and a harpsichord. Tickets were seven shillings six pence. The concert began at six and was followed by supper and a ball, which the advertisement promised would be "free to all Encouragers of the above Scheme, as long as the Ladies stay."

Williamsburg in 1772 was treated to an early version of the Wild West Show when Joseph Faulks gave an exhibition of "riding one, two, and three horses, in many different attitudes." In the same year theatrical entertainment in Virginia reached a point which has probably never been equalled since, in a performance advertised as follows:

By AUTHORITY.

At the THEATRE *in* WILLIAMSBURG, *on* Monday
the 23d *of this instant* (November)
Will be exhibited, by Mr. GARDINER,

A CURIOUS SET OF FIGURES,

richly dressed, four feet high; they are to appear on the
stage as if alive, and will perform a tragic performance,
called

BATEMAN AND HIS GHOST.
LIKEWISE A SET OF
WATERWORKS,

representing the SEA, and all manner of SEA
MONSTERS sporting on the waves. With the
taking of the

HAVANNAH,

with ships, forts, and batteries, continually firing, until
victory crowns the *British* forces; with the appearance
of the two armies. To which will be added, a magnifi-
cent piece of MACHINERY, called

CUPID's PARADISE,

representing seventy odd PILLARS and COLUMNS,
with the appearance of NEPTUNE and AMPHRITRITE,
and music suitable thereto. The whole to conclude with
a magnificant set of FIREWORKS, such as caterine
wheels, *Italian* candles, sea fountains, and sun flowers
with the appearance of the sun and moon in their full
lustre.

Mr. Gardiner will extend himself between two chairs,
and suffer any of the company to break a stone of two
hundred weight on his bare breast.

TICKETS to be had at the THEATRE which are 3s9.
for the BOX, PIT 2s6, and GALLERY 1s3. The performance to begin at 6 o'clock.

Vivant Rex & Regina.

*** No person can be admitted behind the scenes.

N.B. Between the acts will be instrumental music,
consisting of *French* horns and trumpets.

Families living in town not only had the benefit of such spectacular amusements but also could enjoy familiar visits in the afternoon and evening without having to make an expedition. Groups would gather informally to gossip and sing songs and discuss the latest news from London. An enchanting episode that occurred in Williamsburg in the year 1769 was recorded by Anne Blair:

Mrs. Dawson's Family stay'd the Evening with us, and the Coach was at the door to carry them Home by ten o'clock; but every one appearing in great spirits, it was proposed to set at the Step's and Sing a few Song's which was no sooner said than done; while thus we were employ'd, a Candle & Lanthorn was observed to be coming up Street; (except Polly Clayton censuring their ill taste, for having a Candle such a fine Night) no one took any notice of it—till we saw, who ever it was, stopt to listen to our enchanting Notes— each Warbler was immediately silenced; whereupon, the invader to our Melody, call'd out in a most rapturous Voice, Charming! Charming! proceed for God sake, or I go Home directly—no sooner were those words utter'd, than all as with one consent sprung from their Seats, and the Air eccho'd with "pray, Walk in my Lord;" No—indeed, he would not, he would set on the Step's too; so after a few ha, ha's, and being told what all knew—that it was a delightfull Evening, at his desire we strew'd the way over with Flowers &c. &c. till a full half hour was elaps'd, when all retir'd to their respective Homes.

The visitor, Lord Botetourt, was one of the most popular royal governors Virginia ever had. Yet it was only a few years later that the last royal governor, Lord Dunmore, fled from Virginia, taking with him the cordial hatred of the inhabitants and the last shred of British authority in the colony. The American Revolution was already in the cards when Lord Botetourt was swinging his lantern down the Duke of Gloucester Street, and the

The kind of life which a family can live in one room is vastly different from the kind which can be lived in a mansion.

The stone chimney marks this cabin as belonging to the Piedmont. It is located near Warrenton.

*Their walls still announce proudly, even in ruins, that
the men who built them had enjoyed living.*
The ruins of Rosewell.

Revolution was to have disastrous effects on the Virginia that we have been describing. Many of the large plantations suffered heavily from military activities, and with the opening up of the new lands in the west after the war, the great estates in Virginia underwent an economic depression from which they never fully recovered. Although some of the lavishness of the Virginia plantations was later reproduced during the reign of King Cotton in the estates of the Deep South, Virginia had little share in the new prosperity. Yet the memory of elegance lingered in the houses which had once contained Virginia's great colonial families. Today their walls still announce proudly, even in ruins, that the men who built them had enjoyed living.

A NOTE ON THE SOURCES

The largest single body of material used in preparing this volume was the *Virginia Gazette*, all extant copies of which are now available on microfilm. The *Gazette* was useful principally in preparing the third and fourth chapters. In the study of marriage and the bringing up of children, letters and diaries were the chief sources. Unfortunately these do not survive in as large numbers as one might expect. Of those available the most valuable are Philip Fithian's *Journal and Letters* (H. D. Farish ed., Williamsburg, 1943) and William Byrd's *Secret Diary* (Louis B. Wright and Marion Tinling eds., Richmond, 1941). *The Virginia Magazine of History and Biography* (Vols. I-LIX, 1893-1951) and the *William and Mary Quarterly* (First Series, Vols. I-XXVII, 1892-1919; Second Series, Vols. I-XXIII, 1921-1943; Third Series, Vols. I-VIII, 1944-1951) contain a substantial number of eighteenth-century letters scattered through their numerous volumes. A series of valuable documents on education in colonial Virginia is contained in Edgar W. Knight's *A Documentary History of Education in the South before 1860*, Volume I *European Inheritances*, Volume II *Toward Educational Independence* (Chapel Hill, 1949, 1950).

Among the secondary works which deal with the

subject of this monograph by far the best is Julia Cherry Spruill's admirable *Women's Life and Work in the Southern Colonies* (Chapel Hill, 1938). The older works of Alice Morse Earle, *Home Life in Colonial Days* (New York, 1898), *Child Life in Colonial Days* (New York, 1927), and *Colonial Dames and Goodwives* (New York, 1898) are as useful today as when first issued. The servant problem in colonial America is dealt with in Abbot E. Smith, *Colonists in Bondage* (Chapel Hill, 1947), and the family life of slaves in E. Franklin Frazier, *The Negro Family in the United States* (Chicago, 1939). Louis Morton's *Robert Carter of Nomini Hall* (Williamsburg, 1941) gives many glimpses of the home life of a typical large planter. For other aspects of Virginia's social history the best account is Mary Newton Stanard's *Colonial Virginia, Its People and Customs* (Philadelphia, 1917).

A fully annotated copy of this monograph is on file in the Research Archives at Colonial Williamsburg, where it may be consulted by anyone who wishes to track down the origins of quotations.

INDEX